Play Pen

Play Pen

New Children's
Book Illustration

Laurence King Publishing

7th July, 2008
84050000290841

LAURENCE KING

© text 2007 Martin Salisbury
Published in 2007 by Laurence King Publishing Ltd
4th Floor
361–373 City Road
London EC1V 1LR
Tel: + 44 20 7841 6900
Fax: + 44 20 7841 6910
email: enquiries@laurenceking.co.uk
www.laurenceking.co.uk

© 2007 Laurence King Publishing
This book was designed and produced by Laurence King Publishing
Ltd, London

A catalogue record for this book is available from the British Library.

ISBN-13: 978 1 85669 524 4

Designed by MARC&ANNA
Assistant editor: Pam Smy
Printed in China

Contents

Introduction

In an age when our daily lives involve the consumption of a feast of increasingly complex and sophisticated imagery, bombarding us from all directions, it is perhaps not surprising that the art of illustration for children has undergone something of a revolution. Existing as it does, quietly out of sight of most adults, this secret world has in recent years seen the arrival of a range of highly inventive graphic artists, working through a rich variety of media - traditional, digital and a mixture of the two - to complement the work of the more established artists in this fascinating field of creative endeavour.

In making what must of necessity be a highly subjective selection, the aim of this book has been to represent a broad range of stylistic and conceptual trends and a range of cultural characteristics from around the world, across what is increasingly a global market. In recent years the field of children's book illustration has attracted an expanding range of artists, drawn to the area by the potential for authorial creative design and by the elevated status of artists working in picturebooks (it would appear that it's no longer uncool). While the breadth and depth of innovation and technique currently visible is breathtaking, it is important to remember that all of this work shares, or should share, a common purpose or prerequisite, namely that it must communicate with and engage the eyes and minds of children. There is much debate about what constitutes an 'appropriate' visual diet for children. It seems that different cultures still have widely divergent views and traditions here. A tour of the annual Bologna Children's Book Fair, for instance, reveals that, at present, UK publishers are deeply conservative in their use of illustration as compared to, for example, their French, Italian, Norwegian, German and Scandinavian counterparts. When asked about this, most UK publishers will claim that, much as they love the 'sophisticated stuff', they can't sell it. It is never easy to know who is leading whom here, but it is hard to believe that some countries produce innately more sophisticated and visually discerning children. A more plausible explanation perhaps lies in a tendency towards the self-fulfilling prophecy approach to marketing.

The term 'visual literacy' has found itself in increasing currency in recent years and is regularly used in relation to children and picturebooks or 'visual texts'. It is a term that seems to have been hijacked by academics. If 'literacy' means the ability to read, write and understand, it seems reasonable that 'visual literacy' might refer to an ability to see, draw and derive aesthetic understanding, rather than an ability to 'decode' pictures into word-meaning in a literal sense. Pictures in picturebooks will mean many things to children. Often the pictures themselves are the meaning now, rather than a mere subservient clue to the meaning of words. And besides, I would argue that pictures in picturebooks have a far more important role to play in the development of the child than a mere aid to reading. As Walter Herdeg pointed out 30 years ago in a special issue of *Graphis** devoted to children's book illustration: 'The smallest owner of books has his special, private art gallery and a unique relationship to it, for he pores over his favourites endlessly, staring at them with a fascination that guarantees indelible memories of scenes and subjects - French, Swedish, Swiss, English, and many others.' Whatever one's views on the stylistic appropriateness of imagery for age-groups, it is surely important that children are exposed to good art. And, increasingly, illustration in children's books is becoming the home of the highest quality art and design.

The revolution in illustrated books for children has not come without concerns and criticisms. To what extent, for instance, are books being used as an indulgent platform for artists ahead of concerns for their audience? And then there is the age-old question of whether highly inventive illustration actually restricts or inhibits the child's imagination. It is perhaps true also that rather too many mediocre picturebooks have been published in recent years. As a result, many publishers are now restricting their lists as booksellers become increasingly selective. Another concern is the effect of the global market on the cultural identities and traditions of illustrated books from around the world. The rich diversity of artwork from across the globe is increasingly threatened by the growing necessity for publishers to sell co-editions of their books to other countries, most importantly the USA. This has initiated a worrying tendency for artists to be given long lists of 'dos and don'ts' and being encouraged to avoid overtly 'local' visual references. This would seem to be a misguided idea, and as the influential writer on children's literature, Joseph H. Schwarcz** pointed out: 'It is fortunately true, though, that as in all good art the universal significance found in the most excellent examples arises from a background with a strong local flavour.'

Some of these issues and questions are explored in depth in academic literature, where the verbal and visual texts of children's books are examined with specific regard to their role in the educational development of the child. This book is more concerned with the art itself, and with the thoughts and motivations of the artists themselves. It is perhaps important to bear in mind that many of the artists do not restrict themselves to working only within children's books. The majority are working across a range of graphic arts areas, including editorial work, design and advertising. Increasingly, children's book illustrators are likely also to be exhibiting in galleries and entrepreneurially creating outlets for their work. It has been interesting to learn through speaking to the various artists represented here that most profess not to consciously consider the age of their audience when creating a book. Shaun Tan expresses this well in his essay, 'Picturebooks: Who Are They For?' (www.shauntan.net):

. . . it's not something I think about much when I'm working alone in a small studio, quite removed from any audience at all. In fact, few things could be more distracting in trying to express an idea well enough to myself than having to consider how readers might react!

It is often claimed that artists in general tend to be more in touch with 'the child within' than most (Serge Bloch speaks eloquently on the subject in discussing his approach to his work). Certainly, playfulness can be a key component of creative experiment. It may then be inevitable, essential even, that the artist-author concentrates on the intuitive creative idea, leaving others to analyze issues of audience age and stylistic suitability. Nevertheless, working in picturebooks does require a highly developed understanding of visual sequence, pace, rhythm and the drama of the turning page.

The selection of artists in the following pages will be as notable for its omissions as for its inclusions. I am mindful too that the concept of 'new' is a rather slippery one, and there is no intention here to suggest or identify any particular stylistic trends. Newness is, of course, inherent in all creative work and is particularly apparent in the ever-inventive output of such brilliant, long-established artists as Maurice Sendak, Quentin Blake, Eric Carle and Satoshi Kitamura. It remains to be seen how many of the newer artists will enjoy such long careers in publishing as these more familiar, established names.

Much has been made of the 'digital revolution' in recent years and its impact on the world of illustration. In the 1980s there was a great deal of talk of 'the end of print', and the decline of the book. As with the arrival of any new technology, overreaction and extravagant, apocalyptic prediction tend eventually to give way to peaceful coexistence. The book as a physical form appears to be in rude health. As yet, we have not seen a high incidence of leather-bound laptops for bedtime reading. It has also been interesting to note that the proportion of overtly digital illustration in children's books seems to have declined in recent years, while its use as an unseen tool has greatly increased. Paradoxically, at a time when almost any form of original artwork can be beautifully reproduced, many now use the technology to make reference to the print effects of an earlier age, or to allow greater control of the design process. It is ironic that so many artists now employ the digital tool to create a raw, 'friendly' aesthetic, often scanning and manipulating the hand-made mark. Almost without exception, artists in these pages who work primarily in front of a screen pointed out that, by preference, they use as few digital tools as possible. Norwegian artist Stian

Hole is interesting here. He speculates about whether his work created using Photoshop will look as dated in the future as 1970s/'80s airbrush imagery does today. I would like to think not. The early days of Photoshop were dominated by the layering aesthetic, as so many designers were infatuated with the new toy. But where the artistic vision drives the work, the tool becomes less and less visible.

'Style', in the context of illustration, is a much-used and rather reductive word. Where 'style' has been self-consciously pursued, the outcome is invariably trite. Recognizable identities inevitably evolve in illustrators' work through the honest toil of trying to express an idea. As Serge Bloch observes, 'No idea, no drawing. Style is not my cup of tea . . . it slows the idea down.' But children are now growing up able instantly to recognize the work of individual illustrators, whose names they know as well as they do those of their favourite writers. And more and more galleries are specializing in the sale of original artwork for illustration, an important extra source of income for the many highly acclaimed but not over-rewarded artists, or at least those whose work is generated through traditional media.

A long-overdue recognition seems to be coming the way of a corner of the graphic arts whose exponents work with quiet integrity, rarely seeking attention or publicity. Perhaps it is time that more of them emerge, blinking, into the daylight to receive the attention and credit they deserve.

Graphis No 177 Volume 31 1975/76. The Graphis Press, Zurich.

**Ways of the Illustrator: Visual Communication in Children's Literature* (American Library Association, Chicago, 1982).

Picturebooks, board books

The picturebook is perhaps the most familiar showcase for the art of illustration for children, hence the disproportionate size of this section of this book. Normally regarded as suitable for three- to seven-year-olds, it is a book whose content and meaning is communicated primarily through pictures, working in tandem with a few supporting words. Increasingly, picturebooks are authored by the artist, the word and image relationship or synthesis being considered from the outset and being crucial to the book's success. Recently, greater importance has been attached to the role of the image in educational development. 'Visual thinking' has become a recognized term. Whereas in the past pictures in picturebooks would often tend to duplicate the verbal text in an 'in case you didn't understand the words, here's a picture' sort of way, increasingly, the relationship is complex, subtle, ironic or subversive. Nevertheless, it is still sadly the case that many picturebooks continue to be reviewed in terms of their word content, with little more than 'brilliantly illustrated' describing the pictorial text. In a picturebook it is often the case that neither the words nor the pictures would make much sense if consumed in isolation. 'A rhythmic syncopation of words and pictures' is Maurice Sendak's definitive definition of this relationship. Occasionally, we have wordless books, where the entire meaning is expressed as a 'visual text'. Quentin Blake's *Clown* is a good example.

The picturebook traditionally comes in a 32- or 24-page format, the binding requirements dictating a number of pages that must normally fall in multiples of eight. The challenge of creating a complete, rounded visual and verbal experience within these constraints is one to which an increasing number and range of artists is drawn. It is often said that the process of authoring a picturebook is most akin to that of directing a film, with the artist also taking responsibility for storyboarding, set design, character casting, writing the screen play and anything else you can think of. But the beauty of the picturebook from the reader's point of view is that it can be 'read' at whatever speed you like. Each page can be returned to, reflected upon and studied at a pace that is not dictated by technology. The verbal text, for pre-readers, may be experienced as a sound track as the book is consumed in the company of an adult. As the text-image relationship becomes ever more sophisticated, so does the growing use of text as image. Despite the widespread practice of printing all text in pure black in order to allow for cheaper reprints in foreign languages, the current interest in hand-rendered letterforms and integrated type and image is encouraging more and more artists to take greater control of the overall design of the book, and to create a visual fusion of word and image on the page. Particularly influential exponents have been Lane Smith (working with designer Molly Leach), Jeff Fisher and Jonny Hannah.

A vast range of stylistic approaches, visual/cultural references and uses of media can be found, as we might expect, in picturebooks from around the world. A few years ago, with the advent of instant worldwide communication, it was beginning to look as though bland homogeny would take over the world of picturebooks, as countries that had previously been isolated, with strong indigenous graphic traditions, enthusiastically imported all things Western and 'Disneyfied' their design for children. Happily, it appears that an awareness of this folly is already reversing the trend as a pride in individual cultural traditions reasserts itself. Pockets of excellence can be found all over the world, with particularly exciting visual traditions continuing in places such as Korea, Iran and the Scandinavian countries. Some countries clearly have less rigid ideas than others about which age-groups are allowed to consume pictures in their books and about what they might contain. In Norway, for example, picturebooks are regarded as suitable for all ages. In Scandinavia generally, there seems to be far less of a preoccupation with protecting children from all things dark and worrisome. In some parts of the world it is taken as gospel that children must have a diet of very bright colours and strong contrast. In others, pictures in picturebooks naturally reflect the artistic or painterly concerns of their particular national heritage. Some countries import and translate the majority of their books. Others are largely self-contained in their publishing habits. A welcome global phenomenon is the all-round improvement in standards of design and production in picturebooks recently, with far greater attention being paid to the tactile, aesthetic quality of the book as an object.

brian biggs

Brian Biggs grew up in the suburbs of Houston, Texas, which is not, perhaps, the most likely environment for a self-confessed Europhile. Speaking of these early years he says: 'I always felt that there was something missing. I was curious about European culture. I watched French films a lot. Later, when I went to France, everything seemed to fall into place.' It is perhaps unsurprising, then, that Brian Biggs was the first American to illustrate for the highly influential French publishers, Éditions du Rouergue. The book in question, *Un Mode de Transport*, in the Touzazimute series, is a playful exploration of the world of transport. It culminates with a hilarious schematic pictorial journey that carries the reader from birth to death through the metaphor of age-appropriate vehicles. The book overflows with graphic wit and charm that engage and amuse readers of all ages.

Biggs studied graphic design at Parsons School of Design in New York City and then studied for a year in Paris. His early career as an artist was spent mainly doing editorial work and comics but he explains, 'The bottom fell out of the editorial market. I couldn't compete with photography. And of course comics don't make any money. My income disappeared and I found myself waiting tables at thirty-five with a family to support. My clients had been mainly in Silicon Valley. We moved from San Francisco to Philadelphia and I decided to completely review my portfolio. It was a case of necessity being the mother of invention. I threw out all the crap and kept the good stuff. And I sent dummy books to some of the top publishers. Knopf/Random House came back to me and that's how the "Shredderman" books eventually came about. Initially, they particularly liked a drawing I had done of a baby on a unicycle. We have talked about a book about babies going somewhere, a project that I still hope to work on'.

Now he feels very at home in the world of children's books. Unlike the editorial world, he says, children's book publishers are interested in seeing new things, new approaches. 'It's a very creative area. With people like Sara Fanelli and Alexis Deacon working in the field, it's very exciting at the moment.' In terms of content, he says he enjoys working with anything that's well written: 'I try to avoid thinking too consciously about the fact that I am making pictures for children. I also avoid looking at other children's books too much. I don't want to be pigeonholed. My agent always says "just concentrate on your story - we'll figure out what to do with it".'

Biggs has taught Illustration at a number of art schools, an activity he thoroughly enjoys. 'I love teaching,' he says, 'It gives me ideas. Originally it was something I did out of necessity, but I value it greatly.' He is also, like so many illustrators, a musician. 'I play the accordion. I often play it at Lane Smith's book signings. He hates it.'

1
Double-page spread from *Un Mode de Transport* (Éditions du Rouergue, Touzazimute series, 2004), in which Biggs' playful artwork references both American and European comic traditions.

1

2–3
Further spreads from *Un Mode de Transport*. Hand-drawn line combines with sensitive digital colouring.

4
Cover for *Un Mode de Transport*. Biggs is the only American to have contributed to the innovative and influential Touzazimute series for French publishers, Éditions du Rouergue.

4

marc boutavant

A difficult-to-pull-off combination of 'retro chic' and genuine warmth characterizes the work of Frenchman Marc Boutavant. Born and brought up in rural Burgundy, he now lives and works close to Gare du Nord in Paris, a location that provides easy access to London where his representing agency, Heart, is based. His education involved a Baccalauréat D, which was 'in the direction of biology', followed by two years at art/communication school, an experience which, charmingly, he describes as 'Nothing special, I think, but a chance for me to leave the village.'

Boutavant's stylish illustration work has come to prominence in recent years through books such as *Another Night Before Christmas* (written by Carol Anne Duffy, John Murray, 2005). The work is produced entirely digitally and Boutavant cites the discovery of the Wacom tablet as a key influence in the development of his visual vocabulary: 'I used to work late into the night with a zero pencil and acrylic paints but one day, suddenly, I was free. I could construct shapes and colours, move them about and do what I wanted with them. Perhaps I no longer had such a "seductive" medium but I had to find a way to make it seductive. And the great thing was, I was no longer looking at the end of my finger. My hand was drawing but my eyes were looking only at what I was drawing. It made me raise my nose from the paper. Of course, beyond the technical, the biggest influence on work is life. My own children play an important part in feeding the work too . . . intangible things, little smiles or things like that.' He works entirely in Photoshop using 'as few tools as possible'. On the subject of style, he says that in the past he was concerned that too much self-awareness in terms of the visual identity or stylistic qualities in his work would be destructive; that 'knowing more would be bad for inspiration', but he now feels able to 'grow in it and make it grow'. Boutavant says that he doesn't consciously think differently when illustrating for children as distinct from general illustration work, but he talks of the more demanding and sometimes exhausting nature of book illustration, using the metaphor of '. . . bags that take time to empty. Children's books wash me up a bit more. Sometimes I can feel empty before the end of it!'

1

2

3

1
Cover for *Le Sapin* ('The Pine Tree', written by Hans Christian Andersen, Nathan Jeunesse, 2005). Boutavant manages to bring a friendly, organic feel to his illustrations through a painterly use of digital media.

2
'Abracadabra', a design for a jigsaw (Nathan Jeunesse, 2005). A richly decorative design, full of humorous anecdotal detail.

3
A double-page spread from *Mouk S'Ennuie un Peu* ('Mouk is a Little Bored', Éditions Mila, 2003). Simple hand-rendered lettering sits comfortably here with an economical use of line.

4 (overleaf)
From *Le Tour de Mouk* ('Mouk's Journey', Albin Michel Jeunesse, 2007). A tour-de-force illustration in which every one of Boutavant's characters has a distinctive and convincing sense of personality.

alexis deacon

Alexis Deacon burst onto the children's book scene in 2002 with *Slow Loris* (Hutchinson), a brilliant debut that grew from a project begun while he was still an art student at Brighton University in England. The book instantly stood out from others by recent graduates because of the maturity of draughtsmanship, characterization and humour. The follow-up for the same publisher in 2003, *Beegu*, confirmed his brilliance. Selected by *The New York Times* as one of the ten best children's books of the year and shortlisted for the prestigious Kate Greenaway award, *Beegu* revealed more of Deacon's range as both artist and author with its poignant depiction of loneliness and isolation through the character of a young alien creature, lost in an uncaring world.

Deacon speaks passionately about the importance of draughtsmanship. *Slow Loris* evolved from what had initially been a very different concept. He had been trying to draw various monsters from imagination and made a visit to the zoo to gain inspiration from observation. It was through that process of observation that he began to realize how much there was to learn from the natural world. A compulsive drawer and filler of sketchbooks, Deacon now uses small-scale pencil drawings, enlarged on a photocopier, rearranged, recopied onto good-quality paper and coloured with watercolour and gouache. Sometimes he uses a layer of linseed oil to seal an image and rework it. This enhances the hazy, ethereal quality that often characterizes his work.

Jitterbug Jam (written by Barbara Jean Hicks, Hutchinson, 2004) showed that Deacon could work successfully with other authors and with a much more complicated approach to text/image narration. This book also made *The New York Times* top ten.

The word 'charm' is perhaps overused in relation to children's books and sometimes refers to the antithesis of such a quality - sentimentality. In fact, charm is a rare commodity in this field. Deacon's work has it in abundance. Graphically, the imagery manages to combine classic traditions of English book illustration with a clearly contemporary feel.

Barbara Jean Hicks ♣ Alexis Deacon

Jitterbug Jam

A Monster Tale

1

1–3
Cover and inside pages from *Jitterbug Jam* (written by Barbara Jean Hicks, Hutchinson, 2004). Deacon's drawings never seem to be overworked, their freshness bringing the most unlikely of creatures to life.

So out I come.

No orange-headed boy about to show his face
with Boo-Dad round, nohow –
Boo-Dad the *biggest, baddest*
monster grampa ever.

Hey, Bobo!

And Boo-Dad grabs me up in a great big monster hug,
and before you say lickety-split 'n' spit-fish . . .

everyone's swiggin' hot bug juice

and scarfin' big old monster slabs of homemade bread with jitterbug jam
like they been starved since half past June!

Boo-Dad asks me how I been, and I tell him,

Good mostly—
not counting the scary boy
underneath my bed.

Then what does Boo-Dad
do but scoop up me and
Buster and plop us down
on his big old monster
knees and start in on a
story about the olden days,
just like always.

2

3

4

But what's this?
A new toy?

5

6

And when the sun comes up,
we use our last bit of strength
to crawl back to our places.

7

4–8
Cover and spreads from *While You Are Sleeping* (Hutchinson, 2005). Draughtsmanship of the highest quality underpins Deacon's work. The familiar theme of toys coming to life after dark is here given fresh life through superb characterization and movement.

8

stian hole

'I think children are now far more experienced in visual reading than in the past', says Stian Hole, whose richly atmospheric and deeply Nordic imagery is created digitally. The illustrations are made as layered montages in Photoshop. 'I collect textures, digital photos, scans, notes and sketches. In Photoshop I rearrange, scale and flip them until, hopefully, something interesting happens.' Hole says that he is conscious of the dangers of the 'tool' dominating the aesthetic of the outcome and strives to avoid this: '. . . though I guess they will look just like Photoshop montages ten years from now, just like airbrushed illustrations from the early 1980s . . . you will always be able to trace the tool in the illustrations. But, like my teacher, Bernard Blatch, always said, "The thinking comes first". For me, Photoshop is a very practical and useful tool to express what I want. No more, no less.'

He graduated with a Masters from the Institute of Visual Arts in the National College of Art and Design (SHKS) in Oslo, Norway (1991-96) after two years spent in the army on the Norwegian-Russian border. His first children's book, *The Old Man and the Whale* (Cappelen, 2005), evolved when Hole was living in Kvaefjord in the northern part of Norway. This is a tale of two estranged, feuding brothers who are reconciled by strange circumstances. 'The illustrations, which I guess are influenced by the wonderful northern landscape, came first, then the text.' He also cites the music of Swedish singer-songwriter Ulf Lundell as an influence on this book. The publishers Samlaget and Cappelen and, in particular, editor Ellen Seip at the latter have played an important role, Hole says, in the development and encouragement of high-quality, innovative picturebooks in Norway.

Garmann's Summer, also published by Cappelen, is similarly infused with a rich sense of place but this time influenced by the author's journey to Cape Cod on the coast of Massachusetts and by the work of his favourite painter, Edward Hopper. Also, he says, he is fascinated by Holden Caulfield, the protagonist of J. D. Salinger's *Catcher in the Rye*.

Hole says that he doesn't spend too much time thinking about the reader's age: 'I try to tell the story right. My experience is that children don't fear what they don't understand. Making picturebooks is a way of sharpening my senses. I feel very happy and concentrated when I work on these projects. I step into another world where I am God. I learn to love new people. I love Cornelius [from *The Old Man and the Whale*] and now also Garmann. They live inside my head.'

Garmann's Summer was awarded the Bologna Ragazzi Award for fiction in 2007.

1

og hører hvordan
...gen. De slår hendene
...ndre og virrer som bier
...g grønne fingre!» sier
...r at «nå får du roser i
... Blomster har navn som
...an hører på tantene:
...ntemum, Tagetes
...ann og pappa lage

1 (previous page)
Double-page spread from *Garmanns Sommer* (Cappelen, 2006). The medium of digital photo-collage does not overwhelm the sense of place that emerges strongly from the artist's designs.

2–3
Cover and spread from *Garmanns Sommer* .

4–5
Double-page spreads from *Den Gamle Mannen og Hvalen* ('The Old Man and the Whale', Cappelen, 2005).

2

3

4

5

meng-chia lai

Originally from Taiwan, Meng-Chia Lai studied illustration at Cambridge School of Art, Anglia Ruskin University in England, followed by a Masters in Communication Art and Design at the Royal College of Art in London. The ebullience of her ideas, and the warmth and humanity in her work quickly won her publishing contracts while still studying at undergraduate level. A genuinely child-like vision is coupled with a sophisticated sense of colour, design and story telling. *Peebi se Perd* ('Peebi Gets Lost', Lirabelle, 2006) gently addresses the familiar issue of a child's short attention span leading him into trouble. Resolving not to lose sight of his dad in a busy world of other grown-ups, he is quickly distracted, with the inevitable consequences. *Oh!* (2007) is also published by Lirabelle of France and demonstrates the same authorial awareness of a child's take on reality. This book deals with the literal way in which a child understands a mother's exhortation not to swallow an orange pip because 'a tree will grow inside you'. The artist's cultural origins are more apparent here in a series of simple line drawings with a strongly classical Eastern flavour: limited colour on textured, absorbent paper heightening the effect.

Meng-Chia Lai works with a wide range of media, almost all non-digital. Despite this, a strong sense of identity flows from the work, which is underpinned by a period spent studying traditional Chinese techniques in watercolour and oil: 'Then, studying in England, I was encouraged to play and experiment more, mixing different media and having fun. I only use the computer when I have to!' She cites the work of Picasso as a major influence, particularly his line and his print work. 'Also, like most artists, I can be influenced by small aspects of other people's work - the way someone uses colour or applies paint. But I am mainly influenced by the things I see - everyday things, little experiences - and primarily by my store of memory.'

Meng-Chia Lai says that, as a child, she enjoyed reading traditional Chinese stories more than the many books that were translated from European languages. One of the major differences that she notices between Eastern and Western books for children is the greater attention to 'message' in the former: 'Many of the books that I grew up with contained strong messages for children about how to behave well, how to be respectful towards older people. European books seem to be based more in fantasy and imagination. In Taiwan the books are more related to experience.'

1

2

1–8
Cover design and interior spreads from *Oh!* (Lirabelle, 2007). A deceptively child-like graphic technique coupled with genuine empathy with the fears and concerns of children give Meng-Chia Lai's work great charm.

Don't talk
with your mouth full.

3

'Wen, are you alright?' Mei asks me.
Now all my classmates come.
'Wen, are you OK?'
'Uhm, I just swallowed an orange pip.'

4

'We have less and less trees
on earth. To protect our earth,
we need to have more trees,'
Miss Wang said,

I want to protect our earth,
but I don't want to become an orange tree.

I worry all afternoon.
I don't want to
become an orange tree.

5

6

I don't want to become an orange tree.

'Look! It's an orange tree!' Mei shouts.
'Hey! Guys! I am Wen! Over here!
My classmates don't recognise me.
And they don't seem to hear my voice.

I am Wen! Hey! Over here!

paula metcalf

Paula Metcalf first came to prominence when her work was exhibited as one of the Highly Commended entries in the Macmillan Prize for Children's Picturebook Illustration. This led to a publishing contract with Macmillan Children's Books. She had previously authored *Norma No Friends* for Barefoot Books in 1999, while still an undergraduate student at Cambridge School of Art in England. On completing her Masters in Children's Book Illustration at the same institution, *Mabel's Magical Garden*, produced as her final project, was published by Macmillan.

As a storyteller, Paula has extraordinary breadth, her subject-matter ranging from the comical to the lyrical, but always underpinned by a rich sense of humanity, warmth and personality. Early work showed the importance of Eastern European graphic traditions as an influence. She had spent some time working in Slovakia and also studied the Russian language. The Czech animator and illustrator Jiri Trnka is a particular favourite of hers, along with the great Yuri Norstein from Russia. But the strongest influence on the nature of her work is, she says, her lifelong interest in dance. For many years she harboured a desire to become a dancer. Now she lives out her dancing through her characters, whose movements and gestures are always elegant and poised, and play an important role in the visual narrative. Paula feels that characterization has been an ongoing issue for her: 'I look back at my early work and realize that the characters were perhaps not as "appealing" as they might be. This was something I talked about a lot with publishers. I hope I have managed to make them more friendly without losing my own particular visual identity.'

Another key influence that the artist identifies is the visual culture of the 1970s: 'I think that, in many ways, I am still stuck in my childhood. I grew up in the 1970s and the colours and motifs of the period still seem to dominate my palette.'

1–5
Spreads and endpapers from *Mabel's Magical Garden* (MacMillan, 2005). This book gently cautions the young reader against the dangers of building metaphorical walls around oneself (sunlight won't get in and the flowers won't grow). Motcalf's technique involves detailed tonal drawings on paper that are then developed and coloured digitally.).

...the sun.

1

Mabel's garden was full of flowers. They gleamed in the sunshine.

Every day Nigel and George came to admire them. "I wish we had such beautiful flowers in our garden," said George.

2

3

...thousands of *flowers* ~ everywhere!

"They're so beautiful!" gasped Mabel. "But where did they come from?"

Nobody knew.

...together.

taro miura

Japanese illustrator Taro Miura's distinctively muscular, constructivist children's books have been catching the eye at the Bologna Children's Book Fair in recent years. Miura studied at Osaka University of the Arts, Fine Art Department, where he majored in silk-screen printing. His knowledge of this process is evident in his mastery of the use of flat colour and subtle 'overprinting'. His respect for graphic processes and the traditions of the past is clear. He says, '"Constructivism" is a favourite term of mine. I also like the Japanese idiomatic phrase, *on-ko-chi-shin*, which loosely translates as "new ideas come from knowledge of the past". I think my inspiration comes from old picturebooks, advertising art and modern art. I tend to change my way of working according to the nature of the idea.'

In Miura's first published picturebook, *Je Suis* . . . (La Joie De Lire, 2004), the influence of the great Soviet artists and designers such as El Lissitzky is particularly evident. *Ton* (Edizioni Corraini, 2004) is a book about weight. It cleverly describes in visual terms the different ways people move or carry an object according to how heavy it is. Reminiscent of Soviet political posters of the 1920s and '30s, these flat-colour images combine with crudely powerful, stencilled type to perfectly articulate their meaning. The follow-up to *Ton* is *Tools* (2005), also with Corraini. Tools is a simple but powerful celebration of the shapes of everyday tools and their uses.

Miura works as an illustrator for advertising, magazines and book-cover design as well as in children's books: 'I also work as a graphic designer and have designed most of my own children's books. I began initially by submitting children's book illustrations to the Bologna Illustrators Exhibition.' He now finds the world of children's books particularly stimulating: 'I hope to make more and more picturebooks using whatever methods I find enjoyable.'

1

1–4
Cover and interior illustrations from *Ton* (Edizioni Corraini, 2004). Flat, graphic shapes and utilitarian stencil-style typography characterize Miura's satisfyingly chunky designs.

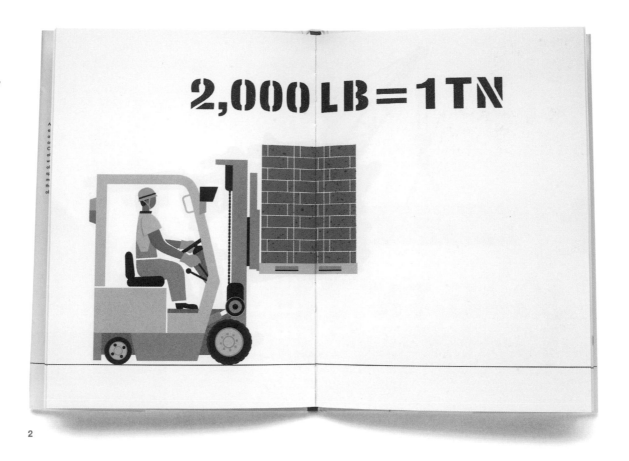

2

3

4

toby morison

After studying at the University of Westminster, London, Morison went on to take his Masters in Illustration at the Royal College of Art in London. During his studies he was already freelancing regularly for leading magazines and newspapers. Editorial work and illustration for design and advertising continued to form the core markets for his creative work, his reputation growing with work for high profile billboard advertising campaigns. He recently relocated to New York and Morison also has close links with France where his work has been widely published. He says, 'As an undergraduate I was obsessed with *the line*. I was always interested in twentieth-century English artists: Ben Nicholson, Edward Bawden, Eric Ravilious and so on. Then I discovered Saul Steinberg. I loved his drawing and his ideas, his graphic wit. This is something I've always been drawn to. André Francois and Jean-Jacques Sempé are other examples.'

Morison's work is characterized by its reverent use of line, the evident fascination for the linear representation of everyday things, bottles, furniture, clothing and so on. His sketchbooks are full of such drawings, lovingly rendered in pencil. Colour is added in flat washes, often playfully referencing the misregistration of print processes. His work is regularly refreshed by drawing trips abroad, in particular to India, a destination and subject that holds a continuing fascination for him.

Little Louis Takes Off (Simon & Schuster, 2007) is Toby Morison's first book for children. 'The idea for the book had been there for some time. The final version emerged with the assistance of my editors at Simon & Schuster who were really helpful.' The book tells the story of a bird who can't fly, and who consequently travels by aeroplane. Visually, this charming book makes reference to the romance of travel, the golden age of travel posters and artists such as Abram Games. 'I also liked the idea of a bird being given peanuts and water on the flight. It's exactly what it would want.' The experience of working on his own children's book has been a pleasant one: 'In editorial work I am used to being asked to "fill a space". With this project it was nice to feel so valued, and to work with people who are taking so much care over the project and valuing what I do.'

1

1–7
Illustrations from *Little Louis Takes Off* (Simon & Schuster, 2007). The unlikely story of a bird who travels by aeroplane is brought to life through imagery that recalls mid-twentieth-century advertising design.

2

3

4

5

6

7

elena odriozola

Born and based in San Sebastian, in the Basque country, Elena Odriozola's work is widely known in her native Spain and is becoming increasingly visible to a wider audience. Her first book in English was *Vegetable Glue* (written by Susan Chandler, Meadsowside, 2004). The publication of *The Opposite* (written by Tom MacRae, Andersen Press, 2006), illustrated by Odriozola, brought further exposure to an English language audience. This clever book playfully and theatrically explores the idea of 'opposite' as a character. The artist successfully combines highly stylized figures and daring use of picture space with a genuine sense of warmth and humour. She says: 'My education didn't really have too much to do with illustration. I studied Art and Decoration. I worked for eight years at a publicity agency and for the last few years in the job I was the art director. I suppose the thing that has influenced me to draw is my background. It was something that I always did as a child. My father and grandfather were both painters.' Her output as an illustrator has, Odriozola says, been exclusively in the field of children's book illustration to date. She is inspired by her own intuitive feelings and everything around her, in particular, she says, 'beauty'. 'I believe the most important thing to me in work is freedom; freedom to express myself. Without that it would be impossible to create a good piece of work.'

1

1–2
From *Begira Begira* ('Look, Look', eight writers, Elkar, 2006), a collection of short stories, poems and puns from the Basque literary tradition. Odriozola combines colour washes with a drawn line and scanned-in texture.

3

4

5

6

3
Illustration entitled 'Descano' ('Pause') from *Fin* ('End', written by Alejandro Fernandández, Autoedition, 2006).

4–6
Illustrations from *The Story of Noah* (written by Stephanie Rosenheim, Meadowside, 2006). The designs for this book have a quiet yet epic presence, with powerful compositions that make the most of long, landscape-shaped format of the book.

7–8
From *Begira Begira* (eight writers, Elkar, 2006).

9–11 (overleaf)
From *Cuando Sale la Luna* ('When the Moon Rises', written by Antonio Ventura, Thule Ediciones, 2006). Powerful composition and understated characterization give these illustrations an unsettling sense of 'otherness'.

12–13 (overleaf)
From *The Opposite* (written by Tom MacRae, Andersen Press, 2006).

7

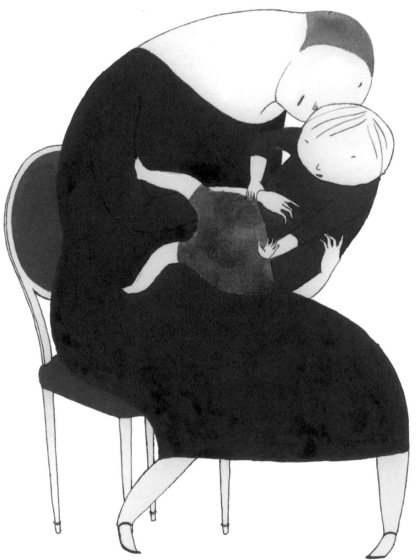

8

9

10

11

12

13

květa pacovská

In *The Art of Květa Pacovská* (North-South Books, 1994), the artist is quoted as saying, 'Why do I draw? Because I need it. Because without drawing I cannot exist. It is like breathing. A drawing is such as it is. It should not and cannot pretend it expresses our feelings and our thoughts.'

Květa Pacovská's unique yet influential presence in the world of children's book illustration has been felt more powerfully in recent decades though she has worked prolifically for many years and is now approaching her eighties. She originally graduated from the Academy of Applied Arts, Prague, in 1952, where she studied painting. A passion for colour and for paper is evident in all of her work for children's books. As Wendy Coates-Smith points out in her essay on Pacovská in *Line No 2* (APU, 2001): 'Her books, which exert a powerful spell on the reader, do so because she is concerned with experiences which are not linked to the visualization of a text - though she is quite capable of doing this - but to a more total experience of the book as a means to link the spirit to the adventure of turning the page.' This interest in the physical and sensual experience of a book pervades all of the work. Dominant vibrant reds are frequently offset by judiciously placed greens and blacks. All aspects of the book's form are controlled by the artist - size, shape, binding, typography etc. Many of her books contain cut-out shapes, holes, folding sections and extended pages. Pacovská has, in many ways, raised the art of the picturebook to new levels. It is fitting that the work of such a respected, senior artist should embody the word 'new' in relation to book art.

1–6
Cover and spreads from *Flying* (North-South Books, 1995). Pacovská's playful sense of adventure is evident in her use of colour and the interaction between the illustrations, the words and the physical form of the book itself.

1

2

3

4

5

6

marina sagona

The highly distinctive colour palette and graphic style of Marina Sagona have recently embraced children's books, adding to a richly varied CV that includes design work for an Issey Miyake collection of bags and shirts, designs for Swatch, murals for Florida's Disney World, animation for television and numerous solo exhibitions in Europe and the US. Sagona was born in Rome and studied at the Institute of Design there but as far as children's books are concerned, she regards herself as self-taught. A feeling that the art of illustration was not regarded as a serious career in her home country of Italy led to a move to New York.

A 1960s screen-print aesthetic pervades Sagona's *NO* (Orecchio Acerbo, 2006), subtitled *Anna et il Cibo* ('Anna and Food'). The highly contemporary vibrant candy colours and partially hand-rendered type serve the artist's simple but effective theme of a child's refusal to find time to eat when there are far too many more important distractions (familiar territory to all parents). Italian publisher Orecchio Acerbo's use of externally mounted cover boards make this an attractive, rustic production.

Sagona clearly enjoys this new creative outlet: 'It is important and stimulating for me to get involved in different kinds of projects but at the moment I find it particularly rewarding to work in children's books. Also, I can now read them to my daughter who is four years old and enjoys them. It is very different from other creative outlets where you are usually under the pressure of a tight deadline and often have to deal with strict art direction. Books give me freedom and time, at least in the early stages, and the luxury of being able to express myself in a more articulate way. But I don't "think differently" when I'm working for children.' On the slippery concept of what is appropriate visually for children and the disparities of view on this in different cultures, Sagona says: 'I think the Americans are much more concerned than Italians about what is or is not suitable, and especially about what would be "politically correct".'

Sagona works initially with gouache and brush, eventually scanning and touching up in Photoshop. She says that, while she still loves the feeling of brush on paper, she is increasingly fascinated by the computer. The unique sense of colour is influenced by living in New York City: '. . . the sharpness of the light and the Minimalist modern art traditions.'

1

1–3
Cover and spreads from *No: Anna e il Cibo* ('No: Anna and Food', Orecchio Acerbo, 2006). The vibrant use of colour suggests a screen-print aesthetic but the illustrations are in fact created using gouache paint.

2

3

E ANDARE NEI PRATI.

4

5

6

È LA RICETTA PER CRESCERE IN FRETTA?

PUÒ DARSI DI SÌ.

7

8

4–8
Further interior spreads from
No: Anna e il Cibo. The influence
of mid-twentieth-century
American art and design can
clearly be seen in Sagona's
work. These references combine
with a highly individual and
contemporary use of colour.

istvan schritter

Istvan Schritter is much more than a brilliant illustrator of books for children. He is a passionate and tireless campaigner for the cultural importance of children's book illustration both in Argentina, where he is based and in the wider world. Alongside his prolific output as an artist, he works as an academic and writer in the field. He is a self-taught artist and puts this into context in relation to the practice of illustration in Argentina: 'Until very recently there was no possibility to study as an illustrator here. That is why most Argentinian illustrators are self-taught. Only five years ago a specialism in illustration was opened at Martín Malharro School of Art in Mar del Plata. I was in charge of the first university-level seminar in children's book illustration at the Instituto Universitario Nacional de Arte de Buenos Aires - Dirección de Posgrado en Artes Visuales "Ernesto de la Cárcova".' Schritter teaches at postgraduate level but notes that there is still no specific degree programme in the country in Illustration. Though he says the situation is improving gradually, he laments the general marginalization of the subject in his country: 'Argentine reviewers of picturebooks are traditionally educated in literature and generally fail to understand or comment on pictures beyond a few superficial qualitative statements such as "the illustrations follow the text".' Through his own efforts in writing numerous journal articles on illustration, presenting a TV series on the subject and, in particular, his book, *Las Ilustraciones en los Libros Para Niños* ('Another Way of Reading: Illustrations in Books for Children' Universidad Nacional del Litoral y Lugar Editorial, 2005), Schritter has raised the profile of illustration in South America.

Much of Schritter's own work is in the form of paper collage produced entirely by hand: 'I never use a computer, except for writing or scanning as a way of recording. I cut everything with a pair of ordinary tailor's scissors, down to the tiniest circle for the tiniest pupil of an eye. The larger pieces are stuck with solid glue and the smaller ones with liquid glue and tweezers. Sometimes there are twenty or twenty-five layers of paper. You can see this in good-quality reproductions where the shadows between layers are visible. I try not to use rulers so that the cut line is not too perfect, giving warmth to the overall image.' Not surprisingly, he describes himself as 'orderly and obsessive'. In contrast to this tiny scale, Schritter has produced giant murals for a number of institutions and events including the Buenos Aires Children's Book Fair and Universidad Pedagógica Nacional de México, working with fabrics, paper and cardboard. 'The challenge is the same,' he says, '. . . to create spaces full of detail.'

Yet another important aspect of his work is his role as editor of a series of picturebooks entitled 'Libros-álbum del Eclipse' (Ediciones del Eclipse). This is the first time that an illustrator has directed a series of books in Argentina.

1

2

1–3
Schritter's dynamic use of colour on white background is achieved through meticulous hand-cut collage.

From *Todo el Dinero del Mundo* ('All the Money in the World', Sudamericana, 2005).

3

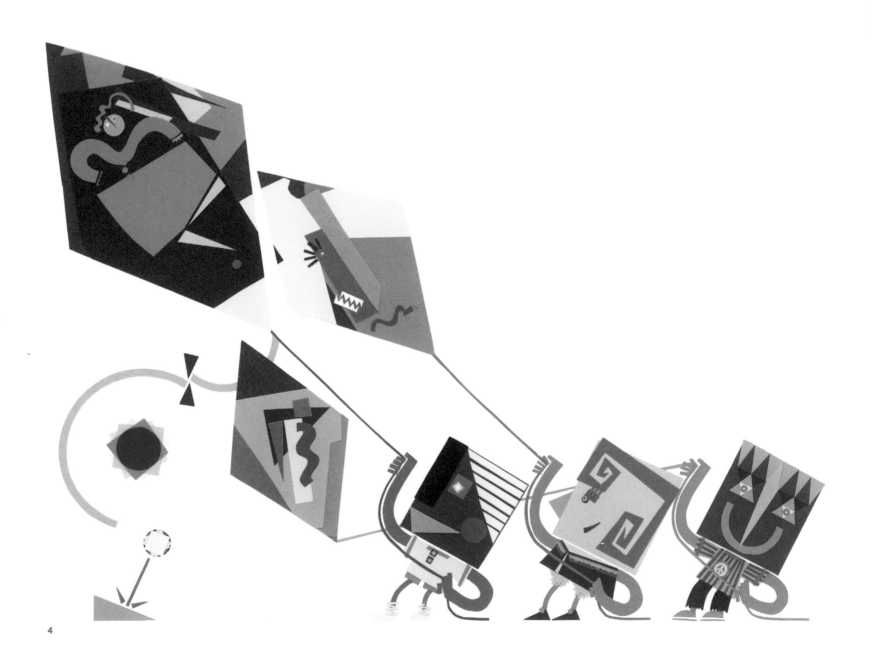

4
From *Ideas Claras de Julito Enamorado* ('Clear Ideas of Julito in Love', Norma, 2000).

5
From *Boca de León* ('Lion's Mouth', EDeBé, 2006).

4

5

6

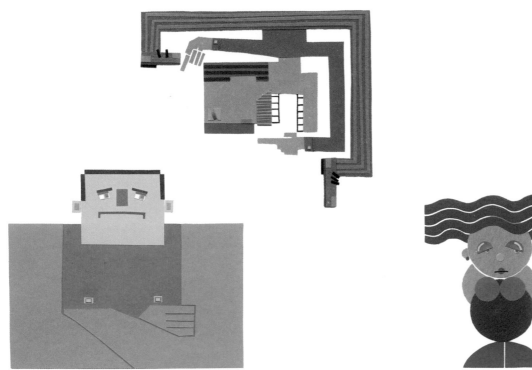

7

6
From *Avión que Va, Avión que Llega* ('Departing plane, arriving plane', written by Laura Devetach, Ediciones del Eclipse, 2007.

7
From *Des Ronds et des Carrés* ('The Circles and the Squares', written by Didier Mounier, Motus, 1998).

8
From *Todo el Dinero del Mundo* (Sudamericana, 2005).

8

j.otto Seibold

J.otto Seibold is one of the most original and influential artists to emerge onto the children's book scene in recent years. One of the first whose artwork was overtly and exclusively digital, Seibold has exerted a considerable influence on the genre. He began using the computer to create artwork with the earliest crude technology in the mid 1980s. He now creates his work primarily with Adobe Illustrator.

Falling clearly into the 'Postmodern' category, San Francisco-based Seibold's work exudes ironic humour and subtle cultural influences. He has also been an important role-model for illustrators by creating a 'Seibold industry' of products and merchandising, retaining creative control and commercial/licensing rights. In an interview with Kim Evans*, he says that, 'proprietary issues are up there with religion and politics for me.'

Seibold made his name with the *Mr Lunch* series, which ran from 1993 to 1996. Working with his wife, writer Vivian Walsh, he built up a prolific output including the *Olive* books, *Going to the Getty*, *Penguin Dreams*, *Gluey* and *Quincy, the Hobby Photographer*. In 2003, he created a tour-de-force pop-up version of *Alice in Wonderland* for Scholastic (New York). These books are adored by children, giving the lie to the popular publishers' notion that digital artwork is 'unfriendly'. Seibold says that many of the characters and stories are based on his own family pets.

As the sleeve notes for *Olive, the Other Reindeer* (Chronicle, 1997) helpfully explain: 'J.otto draws all of the time. He draws on a *computer*, which makes him sort of like a scientist. But he doesn't wake up till noon, which makes him like an *artist*.'

*www.digital-illustration.com.au/culturezone/jot-iv2.html

1

Cover design for *Gluey* (written by Vivian Walsh, Harcourt, 2002). Seibold's influential digital imagery is augmented in this book by innovations such as spot laminate printing, suggesting a shiny trail of snail slime.

1

SHELL
Rx

GLUEY
a snail tale

GLUEY
a snail tale

WALSH ✿ SEIBOLD

All ages

0-15-216620-3

51500>

0152 166205

Harcourt

VIVIAN
WALSH

J. OTTO
SEIBOLD

...the house broke into pieces.

"Not to worry," said Celerina.
"This house will be fixed. It is an overnight kind of magic.
Come back tomorrow morning and you will see."

2

One day while drinking tea, Celerina had a brilliant idea.
"I'll have a party. I'll invite the animals to my house.
I'll serve toast and jam...and then I'll break the plate right
in front of them! Won't they be surprised when it is
magically repaired!"

Celerina started making the invitations.
On each one she drew a picture of her house,
and then painted the letters P A R T Y.

Gluey noticed that the bunny was drawing pictures
of the house over and over again.
"PARTY!" read Gluey.
He wanted to help.
"I'll make the house look its best."

PARTY
at CELERINA BUNNY'S
HOUSE
"an enchanted afternoon
of toast and jam"

The decorations went up on both the inside
and the outside of the house.

3

4

5

ko kyung sook

Gaining a special mention in the 2006 Bologna Ragazzi awards for *Magic Bottles* (Jaimimage, Seoul, 2006) brought Korean artist Ko Kyung Sook to the attention of a wider audience. The jury commented: '*Magic Bottles* uses Archimboldo-type assemblies to describe the expressive potential of apparently ordinary containers that hide much more complex interiors. Behind the masks of this theatrical comedy lies a very different, intricate world: a metaphysical zoo in a dreamlike, Little Nemo world.'

The sheer exuberance and evident joy of paint on paper mark these images out as something special. Born in 1972, Sook graduated from Dankook University in South Korea where she majored in Oriental Painting. She studied Illustration at postgraduate level at Sookmyoung Women's University and became particularly interested in a career in illustration after attending a workshop for those starting out. 'My first commissioned work was for Jaimimage (the publisher of *Magic Bottles*). It was a series of books for older children called 'Class Bag'. After working on three books in that series, I wanted to do something more personal so I spent some time away from commissioned work and developed a new way of working with oil paint and gouache. *Magic Bottles* was the first book using this approach and also the first book that I have both written and illustrated myself. I was lucky enough to win the Bologna award. Recently, I have worked on two further books: *Great Moongchi* and *My Atelier*.'

Ko Kyung Sook says that the field of children's book publishing particularly appeals to her as an artist: 'I've had opportunities to exhibit my work in galleries but I wanted to connect with a wider audience than the limited few who come to an exhibition. I was confident that through illustration I could express my thoughts visually without losing artistic aesthetics.' Like many book illustrators, she says that she does not consciously think of the age of the audience: 'Instead, I call out my inner child and imagine playful thoughts that help me create my own world.' The sensuous nature of the imagery is reflected in the influences that she cites: 'Everyday things like food decorations, the airy feeling of early morning rain, window frames on traditional houses, looking down from above at passers-by. I think these things are turned into art by how we look at them. Although books from around the world show cultural differences, books from England could be said to be uniquely English, books from Japan or the US uniquely Japanese or American, I think overall approaches show no difference between East and West. The significant differences in approach are to do with who the artists are rather than where they come from.'

1

1–3
Cover and interior spreads from
Magic Bottles (Jaimimage, 2006).

그 후, 이런 일 외에는 아무런 일도 일어나지 않았어요.
다행히 경찰이 마법사를 체포했거든요.
마법사는 우리가 동물들과 어울려 살면 더
재미있을 것 같아서 이런 일을 벌였다고 자백했다죠.
동네 가게에 남아 있던 마법에 걸린 병들도
모조리 거두어들여 그 속의 동물들이 있어야 할
곳으로 모두 보내졌다고 합니다.

그런데 아직도 수거하지 못한 병들이 있다고 하니
여러분! 물건 살 때 조심해서 사야 되겠어요.

2

영필이가 시합을 앞두고
시원한 〈케이오 콜라〉를
마시려고 한다면 말려야 돼요.
정말 난처한 일이 생길 수도 있으니까요.

3

미용실 언니가 수림이의 머리를 예쁘게 손질하고
특별히 〈코코코 No.1〉 모발보호제를 뿌려 주려고 합니다.
향기는 정말 좋았는데 그 속에서 나온 것은
"코, 코, 코……"

4

뚝딱뚝딱 쟁그랑 쟁그랑 신나는 병 공장.
이 공장의 주인은 마법사랍니다. 지금 장난기
많은 마법사가 주문을 걸어 알록달록한 병 속에
무언가를 넣고 있어요!

5

4–6
Further spreads from *Magic Bottles*. Ko Kyung Sook's rich, intense use of paint gives a raw, hand-made feel to a book that looks at everyday containers in an imaginative way. Visible brush strokes give texture to the page while lift-the-flap surprises alternate with bold use of light on dark.

정팔이가 오랜만에 목욕을 하겠다고 합니다.
혼자서도 씩씩하게 목욕을 잘 하는군요.
그런데 〈하하 물비누〉를 짜는 순간,
과연 무사히 목욕을 마쳤을까요?

shaun tan

Australian Shaun Tan is not only one of the more imaginative author-artists working in children's books today, he also has a great deal of interest to say on the subject of illustration generally. His fascinating website (www.shauntan.net) includes essays on subjects such as 'Picturebooks: Who Are They For?', as well as detailed descriptions of a range of his projects including murals, character development and the sponsoring of awards for young artists. Born and brought up in Perth, Western Australia, he graduated from the University of Western Australia with joint honours in Fine Arts and English Literature. He says that the course was primarily academic and theoretical rather than practical, but throughout his studies he had been drawing for student magazines and newspapers and 'selling the odd painting . . . I pretty much learned all my current illustration techniques through doing these small jobs.' The interest in science and technology that is so evident in Tan's creative work also led him to consider a career in biotechnology. His work continued to evolve through an ongoing involvement with small-press comic and science-fiction publishers, a notoriously low-paid world kept alive by enthusiasts. 'I knew very little about picturebooks when first asked to illustrate one, and tended to share many people's prejudice that they were exclusively the domain of young children, not an art form that lends itself to much artistic or intellectual sophistication.'

The aesthetic of science-fiction and comic art is often apparent in Tan's picturebooks. They are invariably enigmatic in content, suggesting allegory or prompting myriad interpretations of their open-ended conclusions. *The Red Tree* (Lothian Books, 2001) has been subjected to a great deal of such analysis, its powerful imagery and surreal juxtapositions suggesting, among other things, references to childhood angst and depression. In fact, as the artist himself explains, like most of his books, the idea evolved through visual motifs which appear randomly in his sketchbooks: '. . . the tree itself was a tiny doodle of a tree with 'the red tree' scribbled underneath, that somehow seemed significant in a sea of other small drawings.' Gradually, a sense of meaning emerges visually: 'Writing and painting is very much about trying different things based on hunches and intuition, often in a silly and playful way, and then looking at them critically to see if they make any kind of sense when cast against the backdrop of lived experience. Do imaginary objects stand up as meaningful metaphors? Do they "make sense" on their own, without being pushed? Being an artist is not about manipulating objects or an audience so much as constantly assessing a series of often accidental and mysterious ideas.'

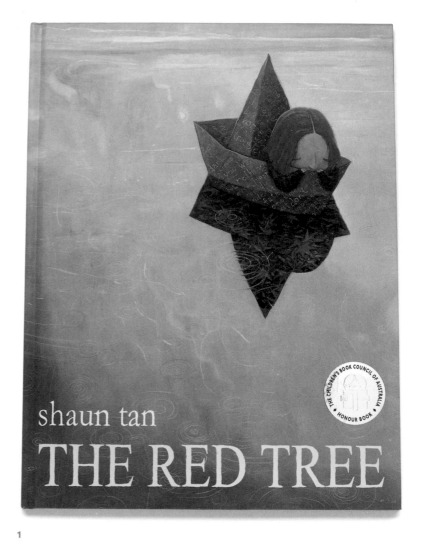

1

1–3
Cover and interior spreads from
The Red Tree (Lothian, 2001).

and things go from bad to worse

2

just as you imagined it would be

3

darkness

overcomes you

4
In this striking spread from *The Red Tree*, Tan uses extremes of scale and surreal juxtaposition to express a powerful sense of despair. Minimal text allows the imagery to do most of the talking.

øyvind torseter

One of a group of highly inventive Norwegian illustrators, Øyvind Torseter initially studied graphic design in his home country before taking a degree in Illustration at Kent Institute of Art and Design in England. His work evidences a clear interest in print, the nature of, as well as the subversion possibilities of registered blocks of colour. He says, 'It was good at college because we had plenty of time to play around and experiment. The college had a great print studio where I could try out lots of things. In my final year I started to use the Mac a lot.' After graduating, he returned to Norway and began working freelance: 'Mostly book-related things, illustrating other people's texts. I also did a lot of personal work that I exhibited. Drawings mostly. I like to tell visual stories and I started to play around with text when I did *Klikk* (Cappelen, 2004).' Torseter feels that the Norwegian illustration scene is particularly interesting at present, notably the area between illustration, graphic design, fine art and cartoons. He also feels that children's books in Norway are not necessarily designed to be exclusively of interest to children. His interests and influences are wide ranging and eclectic: 'I was always interested in cartoons and, as I got older, graphic novels: Will Eisner, Hugo Pratt, Chris Ware's Jimmy Corrigan, Christoffer Nielsen, Tove Jansson's Moomintrolls - the original drawings are beautiful. Also, the fairytale illustrations by Norwegian artist Theodor Kittelsen (very scary) and in no particular order: David Hockney, Max Ernst and Dada, collage, artists' books, outsider art, Jockum Nordström, music, film, animation, fiction.'

Torseter uses a range of techniques but usually those that reflect his interest in print: "I like different printing techniques a lot - etching, silk-screen, lino - I like the limitations of colour that print brings. The illustrations in *Klikk* are first drawn as line drawings then each drawing is colour separated. I draw each area of colour as a separation on paper in pen and black ink so I don't know how it will look at this stage. Then I scan these ink drawings in and layer them in Photoshop and give each a colour. It is really the same as screen-printing. I usually hand-draw everything. When I use the computer it is mainly for colouring and cutting and pasting.'

1

1–3
Cover and interior spreads from *Englefjell* ('Angelmountain', written by Roald Kaldestad, Cappelen, 2006). Individually scanned colour separations are used to create these wistful images.

Der var du jo, smiler ho.
Eg sa jo det, smiler han.

2

Fjella står bratt på alle sider. Svarte skuggar om kvelden. Englefjell er som store, svarte vinger mot den blå nattehimmelen. Frå toppen av fjellet kan ein sjå heile verda. Eller begynnelsen. Ein veit liksom at den vide verda er der ute, over dei fjella, over det havet. Store båtar balanserer på den tynne streken langt der ute. Alt dette som ho og katten såg. Ho står ved vindauget. Suset frå elva er der alltid. Gatelysa står på rekke gjennom bygda.

3

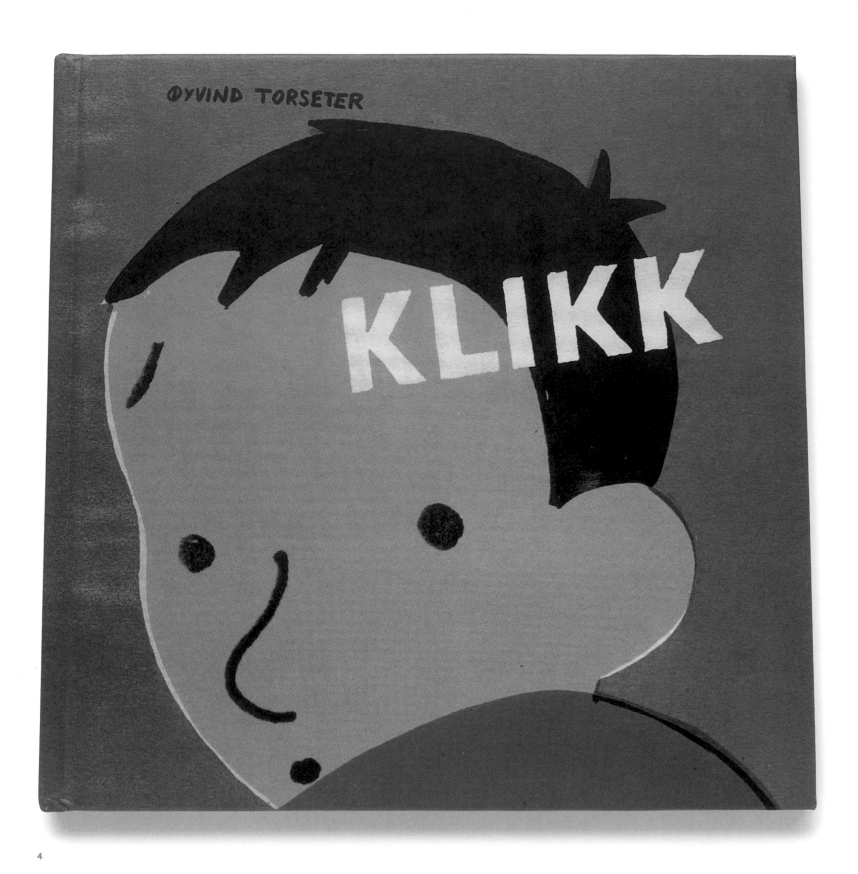

4
Cover for *Klikk* (Cappelen, 2004).
Simple, bold colour separations
evoke early comic reproduction.

5–6
Interior spreads from *For en Neve Havre* ('For a Fist Full of Oats' Cappelen, 2005).

5

6

morteza zahedi

The rich visual culture of Iran is beginning to reach a wider international audience and in recent years the Bologna Children's Book Fair has brought a number of highly original artists from this country to the world's attention. Its long tradition in the decorative and book arts gives Iran a special place in illustration. While some of the formerly isolated countries with rich graphic traditions such as, for example, some of the Eastern European nations, have tended quickly to absorb and embrace the brasher side of Western visual culture, a great deal of Iranian illustration still exudes a sense of its cultural origins.

Morteza Zahedi was born in 1978 in the town of Rasht in northern Iran. There he studied graphics before going to Tehran where he graduated in painting from the Faculty of Art and Architecture. Speaking about the quality and depth of Iranian illustration, he says: 'Maybe this is because before painting, graphic art and literature, in their current form, came to Iran, we already had a culture of book-making and illustrating. The book and the process of book-making have historically been very important. The activity of illustrating was seen as a serious profession.' Despite the quality of the work, illustration in Iran, he says, is not now taken so seriously by all sectors of the artistic community: 'Within the illustration community, yes, but publishers and other branches of the arts do not seem to grant much status to it. Maybe this is because it is seen as only for children. Most publishers are mainly looking to produce cheap books.'

'I am known as an illustrator,' he says, 'but my profession has been mainly as a painter and teacher for many years. I continued illustrating, slowly and seriously, throughout this time. Now, I very much enjoy all three areas of work.' He speaks of the sense of responsibility that an illustrator must have: 'When I take on a new project, I try to look after my conscience. The art of the illustrator is to create something lasting - a permanent artwork. This is not an easy thing to do. Always thinking about new solutions is important to me.'

1

1
From the 'Genie Collection'
series, a personal project, 2005.

2–3
From *Butterfly Journey*
(Shabavaiz, 2006). Zahedi's
highly idiosyncratic graphic style
celebrates the shapes and
patterns made by organic things.

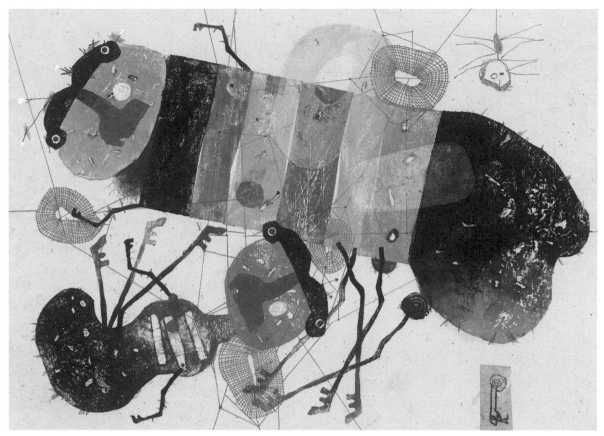

2

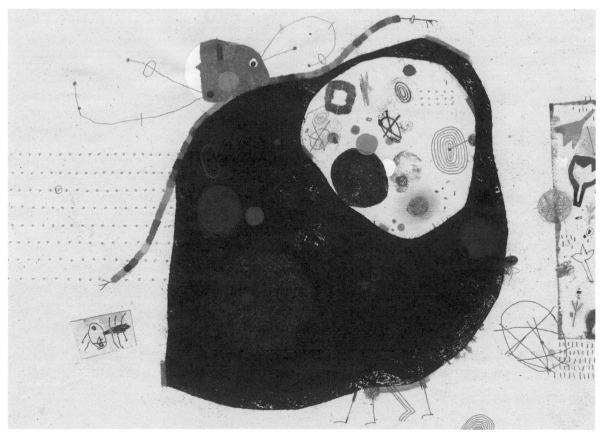

3

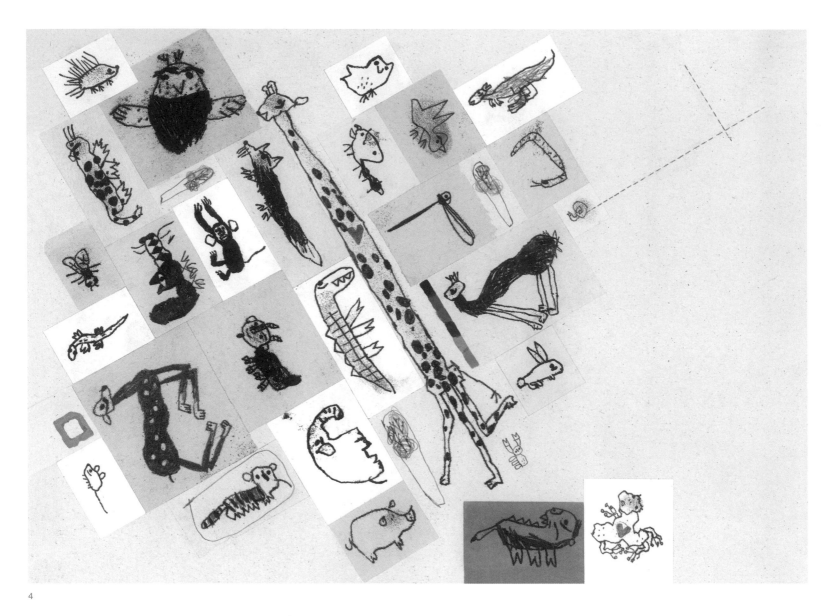

4

4
From *2 Turtles – 2 Humans*
(Shabavaiz, 2006).

5–6
From the 'Rooster Collection',
an experimental series. Personal
experimental work continues to
feed Zahedi's visual vocabulary.

5

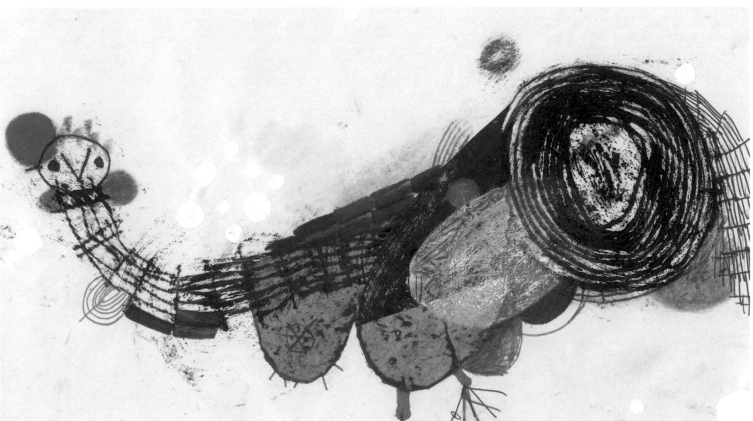

6

Alphabets, wordplay, novelty

This chapter contains a curious little mix of artists and books
that play with words, pictures and perceptions. The illustrated
alphabet is one of the oldest of publishing ideas and yet it is
one that can be reinvented in endlessly original ways. The
earliest chap-books often featured crude illustrated alphabets.
Thomas Bewick's early work included engravings in 1771 for *A New
Lottery Book of Birds and Beasts for Children to Learn Their
Letters by as Soon as They Can Speak*. Children's books tend to
have snappier titles now. Many artists have subsequently enjoyed
the challenge of creating themed alphabet or wordplay books,
from William Nicholson to Brian Wildsmith, Maurice Sendak and
Mitsumasa Anno, the latter's brilliant *Anno's Alphabet: An
Adventure in Imagination* (HarperCollins, 1974) exploring visual
paradoxes and illusions in the manner of the Dutch master of such
wizardry, M. C. Escher. The current revival of interest in the
hand-rendered letterform has precipitated the emergence of a
particularly rich crop of such books, displaying a variety of
approaches to the representation of type and to the word-image
relationship. The majority of these books are artist authored.
This could hardly be otherwise when the fusion of text, image
and overall design form the actual meaning of the book, as
distinct from the narrative, verbal text.

Nursery rhymes and limericks have always played a prominent
role in the children's book, providing a way into the world of
literature in the same way that the pictures form a stepping-
stone to art practice and appreciation. Wordplay and alliteration
can provide not only fun and entertainment but also a helping hand
in registering sounds and shapes in relation to their meanings.
The illustrated alphabet similarly provides a structure that
underpins for the artist an opportunity to thoroughly indulge a
particular preoccupation in terms of content, design and visual
and cultural influence while, once again, providing a window into
the world of letterforms.

Wordless books and books with minimal text convey meaning
pictorially. They can sometimes be demanding to 'read' and
follow, and often contain many hidden references and secondary
narratives that can be pored over and rediscovered by the curious
child. In the Postmodern picturebook subtle references abound
and can be read on many levels, as can be seen in the visual puns
and metaphors in the books shown in this section. The use of
foldout pages and other structural novelties offers further
possibilities in terms of concealment and visual tricks, though
of course these innovations raise production costs.

ragnar aalbu

Born in 1966 in Oppdal, Norway, Aalbu says that he grew up
reading, playing, listening to music, drawing and playing drums
in rural surroundings in the middle of Norway. He was educated
at the National College of Art and Design, Oslo, Norway, at the
Institute of Graphic Design and Illustration (1991-96). His work,
both as author-illustrator and in collaboration with writers
often focuses on visual puns, figures of speech and the visual
side of language: 'I play around with both words and visual ideas
at the same time. Being both author and illustrator is an ideal
situation, as it makes the process smooth and creates a lot of
freedom. The way I approach a book is very different when I work
with a writer. I have to get a feeling for the temper and style
of the text and be respectful in finding a way to visualize it.
Over the years I have learned to trust my intuition so I try not
to think everything through from every angle, but to leave
something unexplained, a sense of uncertainty or room for
coincidence at some level.'

Aalbu cites a number of the 'illustrators' illustrators' as
inspirations - Lane Smith, Sara Fanelli, William Joyce, Maira
Kalman, J.otto Seibold and Peter Sís, and also has a keen
interest in graphic work from the 1930s through to the 1950s.
He works primarily in the field of children's books now, from
time to time also taking on editorial and advertising work and
enjoying the challenge of working for wide-ranging clients and
their different needs.

Aalbu's working process begins with small sketches in pen or
pencil on paper, with watercolour and crayons on top, '. . . very
rough - just to test ideas. When it comes to creating original
artwork, I used to work in acrylics, but over the years I've
worked more and more on the computer. First, I create a digital
drawing. Then I scan in different drawn or painted elements:
paper, wallpaper, patterns, photographs, textures - all sorts.
I use Adobe Photoshop to put everything together as a digital
collage. I try to make illustrations based on simplified forms,
but with rich, organic textures.'

A recent project is *Perler for Svin*, in collaboration with writer
and linguist, Helene Uri (Cappelen, 2006). Translating as 'Pearls
before Swine' (to waste something good on someone who doesn't
appreciate it), it's a book about the imagery of language.
'I visualized the literal meaning of language where words and
sayings are visual.' He says of his own trilogy of domestic
animals: 'The concept is still to present fiction, nonsense,
absurdities and misunderstood facts in a non-fictional way.'
It pleases him greatly that children seem to respond positively
to the books - 'It's great fun visiting schools with my
PowerPoint presentation!'

1
Cover for *Grundig Om Gris*
('Thoroughly Pig', Cappelen,
2005). Aalbu's subtle but
distinctive use of digital colour
is supported by high-quality
production values in this
attractive series.

2
Pages from *Perler for Svin*
('Pearls before Swine', written by
Helene Uri, Mangschou, 2006).
A fascination with wordplay
and visual puns is clear even
to non-Norwegians through
figures of speech that are clearly
international such as 'bookworm'.

3
An example of Aalbu's graphic
yet understated use of imported
pattern and complementary
colour.

2

3

PERLER FOR SVIN

HELENE URI
RAGNAR AALBU

4

4–6
Cover and interior spreads from *Perler for Svin*. More easily translated visual puns and figures of speech are given the Aalbu treatment, with strong references to mid-twentieth-century budget printing techniques.

Revestreker og andre streker

HØNEBLUND · BOKORM · REVESTREK
DATAMUS · LOMMELERKE · ESELØRE
KASTE PERLER FOR SVIN · SKOHORN · LÅR-HØNE
SENNEP SILD · DØD SOM EN SILD · LINSELUS · KUKAKE
KUØYE · KATTEVASK · KUBEIN

SOMMERFUGL · BLEKKSPRUT
TUSENBEIN · EDDERKOPP
SPYFLUE · RUMPETROLL · STEPPEULV
BRENNMANET · BØRSTESVIN · MARIHØNE

jeff fisher

One of the most influential graphic artists of his generation, Jeff Fisher is perhaps best known for his work in editorial and book-jacket design, his iconic cover for *Captain Corelli's Mandolin* (Vintage, 1995) being one of his most familiar designs. Fisher's use of hand-rendered letterforms has played a major part in raising the profile of illustrators as total design authors - that is, illustrators able to deliver complete books and covers without any need for additional typographic design (see also the comments of Pieter Gaudesaboos on page 118). Fisher says, 'I didn't train in graphics, my hand-lettering developed as a way of keeping control of the entire object.' Asked about his influence on the contemporary scene he concedes that, 'Sometimes I do see things that I feel I may have influenced, but then I think of all that went before me.'

Jeff Fisher was born and educated in Melbourne, Australia. He built his practice and reputation working in London from 1983 to 1991, working for a wide range of clients across design, publishing and editorial fields. He has lived and worked in France since 1993. Working in children's books is seen as a natural development alongside his other areas of practice: 'I have always had a fascination for books so the illustrated book is the natural step. I've always enjoyed the process of writing. Illustrators of children's books were probably my first influences: Arthur Rackham and others of that period.'

Fisher's children's books fuse type and image in a painterly, sophisticated yet playful way. Commenting on the overall visual quality of contemporary picturebooks, he says, 'There are good picturebooks out there, you just don't always get to see them. My publisher tells me that this is often the fault of the large booksellers who dictate what is seen.' Like many artists working in children's books, Jeff Fisher avoids conscious concern for the age-group of the audience: 'I have no concept of that thought.'

1

1–3
Cover and interior spreads
from *Pass the Celery, Ellery!*
(Stewart, Tabori & Chang, 2000).

2

3

4

4–5
Cover and interior spreads
from *The Hair Scare*
(Bloomsbury, 2006).

5

martin jarrie

Martin Jarrie is a highly acclaimed artist whose work can be seen in a variety of contexts including galleries, mass-produced posters and leading publications such as *The New Yorker* and the French business magazine *Enjeux*. In *ABC USA* (Sterling Publishing Co., 2005) he brings a Frenchman's eye to American culture with an alphabetical homage to Americana. The book employs the weathered, distressed aesthetic of American 'outsider' or folk art and captures the spirit of the great continent through, among other things, historical events ('D is for Declaration of Independence'), cultural phenomena ('J is for Jazz') and geography ('M is for the Mississippi River'). Layers of acrylic paint are scratched away to allow previously applied colour to emerge, creating a powerful sense of age and history. The rich yet restrained colour gives a dignified finish and a faux-naïve flattening of perspective with schematic arrangement of pictorial information complete the effect.

Born in 1953, Jarrie studied at art school in Angers. After working across a range of outlets in the graphic arts, he settled into a more personal artistic direction in the early 1990s. His distinctively stylized paintings are now widely sold as prints and posters.

1–5

Cover and interior spreads from *ABC USA* (Sterling Juvenile, 2005). The rustic textures of Jarrie's designs give this book a strong sense of the past, while also sitting comfortably within twenty-first-century stylistic trends. Priority is given to arrangement of visual information and colour, with no attempt to create an illusion of spatial depth.

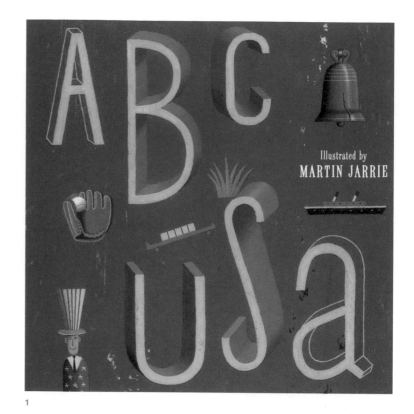

1

2

H is for Hollywood

3

P is for pilgrims

4

T is for tractors

5

david merveille

Le Jacquot de Monsieur Hulot ('Monsieur Hulot's Parrot', 2006) was clearly a labour of love for David Merveille. Published by the influential Toulouse-based purveyors of quality illustration, Éditions du Rouergue, the book pays homage to the great French filmmaker, Jacques Tati.

Merveille studied Graphic Communication under Luc Van Maelderen at L'Ecole Nationale Supérieure des Arts Visuels in Brussels: 'I studied on a five-year course in Graphic Design. In the last two years there was a particular emphasis on illustration and I studied under Josse Goffin, the author of *Oh!* (Éditions Réunion de Musées), which won the Grand Prix at Bologna in 1991. Having trained in design, I take great pleasure in crossing from one discipline to another - design for press, advertising, publishing, posters and so on, but, for me, the children's book is definitely the most creatively stimulating area. Here one can create a personal universe, a graphic identity, a story and, of course, characters.' Though widely published by, for example, publishers such as Milan, Mijade, Nathan, Hachette and Averbode, Merveille says that it is the enlightened editorial policy of Éditions du Rouergue that has really brought out his most personal work: 'They have a very open attitude to authorial content and a highly contemporary vision of children's books. My first book for Rouergue was *Fait Pour Ça* (2004), in which Mr Hulot already made a brief appearance. Then came *Le Jacquot* and now I am working on a third, *Jukebox*.' As a big fan of Jacques Tati, Merveille says that the adaptation of Hulot to book form flowed very naturally for him: 'The silhouette and body language of the character of Hulot translates naturally to paper and of course the starting point was the film posters of Pierre Étaix. But I wanted to reflect Tati's approach to cinema - his concern for detail, his anecdotal observation, interest in everyday objects, his taste in architecture. Also, the little snippets of dialogue and, above all, the visual gags - I wanted to reflect all of this and see how it evolved on paper. Tati's universe has always been close to childhood. Isn't Monsieur Hulot just a grown-up who refuses to grow up? I think Hulot has a seductive power that has crossed generations and I guess I want to prolong this for today's children.'

Le Jacquot de Monsieur Hulot was developed using the following process: 'First, I make a drawing in crayon. Then I trace the drawing onto tracing paper in black crayon. I then scan the drawing in and gradually add colour in Photoshop, with the difficulty of removing the original line. I used to work in chalk pastels but I find that only the computer can give total control over colour and contrast, essential for legibility.'

1

1–3
Cover and interior spreads from
Le Jacquot de Monsieur Hulot
('Mr Hulot's Parrot', Éditions du
Rouergue, 2006).

2

3

4
Each spread of *Le Jacquot de Monsieur Hulot* opens out to reveal a 'what happened next' scenario, nicely translating the filmic humour of Jacques Tati to the page.

kristin roskifte

Talking about her work, Kristin Roskifte says, 'Drawing is the foundation of everything I do. My main tool is my sketchbook. I always take one with me, as naturally as keys and a mobile phone. I constantly record things that I see, hear and think - people, situations, architecture, nature, colour, shapes etc. My library of sketchbooks has become an extensive collection of thoughts and observations. When I get an idea for a project, the first thing I do is flick through some sketchbooks. If I'm lucky, that idea combined with an earlier one can become something new, something that I couldn't have come up with any other way. All my books are results of this process.'

Norwegian artist Roskifte studied in England at Cambridge School of Art, Anglia Ruskin University and Kingston University. Her voracious appetite for visual information informs all of her work. *Still deg I Kø* ('Join the Queue', Cappelen, 2005) is a landscape format book that presents a continuous queue of people, which starts on the cover and ends on the last page. Their final destination is not apparent until the end of book. There are around 260 people in the queue. 'Even if it isn't all visible to the reader, I know stories about everything that I draw in my books. In this book I have an identity for every single person. I know who is happy and who isn't, who does an evening class in ceramics, who has just been dumped by his girlfriend, who is about to have an accident etc.'

In *28 Rom og Kjøkken - Historien om Alf og Beate* ('28 Rooms and a Kitchen: The Story of Alf and Beate', Cappelen, 2004), Roskifte travels through the alphabet via the nooks and crannies of Alf and Beate's house, ingeniously creating letterforms out of the shapes of things. Describing her working method, she says: 'When starting on a book, I make a main story, a "frame" if you like. Within it, I let things happen as I go along. Details are important to me, both because they tell their own stories on different levels and because I like the process of drawing them. This process gives me time to think of underlying stories and new details, as though I am reading the book while I'm making it.'

1

1–3
Cover and interior pages from *28 Rom og Kjøkken* ('28 Rooms and a Kitchen', Cappelen, 2004), in which Roskifte plays with the relationship between letterforms and the three dimensional things that they describe.

2

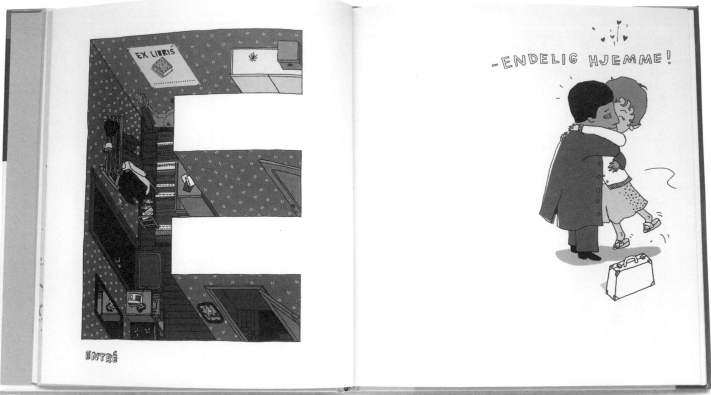

3

4

5

6

4–8
Cover and interior spreads from *Still Deg I Kø!* ('Join the Queue', Cappelen, 2006). An extreme landscape format is used to exploit this visual idea of a continuous line of people.

7

8

harriet russell

Harriet Russell grew up in a twelfth-century priory in Sussex, England, and studied at Glasgow School of Art followed by Central Saint Martins College of Art and Design in London where she took her Masters in Communication Design. Her playfully subversive books, *A is for Rhinoceros* (2005) and *The Utterly Pointless Counting Book* (2004) are published by Edizioni Corraini in Italy. These were both originally developed as student projects. A visit to the Bologna Children's Book Fair persuaded her to approach Corraini, feeling that her work would fit well into their list: 'I had approached English publishers - they liked the books but were not prepared to take the risk of publishing something a bit quirky and alternative! Corraini publish in both English and Italian, which is unusual, I think, for an Italian publisher, but it's a good thing because it makes the books more widely available. I think there are more, smaller, specialist publishers in the rest of Europe who are prepared to take something a bit different.'

Russell says that she enjoys subverting the rules: 'I don't think I would have had nearly as much fun with a straightforward alphabet or counting book! Of course they're not much good as educational aids, but I think children who already know their alphabet and numbers would enjoy the rule-breaking. Also, I don't see my books as being exclusively for children, although they come under that heading. I hope they are more universal. I think they have a gift-book appeal and are appreciated by adults too.' She cites the work of Jonny Hannah, in particular his hand-rendered lettering as a particular influence as a student, along with the great humorists Edward Lear, Edward Gorey and Steven Appleby. Harriet Russell also works in editorial and design publishing, and her book, *Envelopes*, an inventive exploration of rendering postal addresses purely visually, was recently published by Random House (2005).

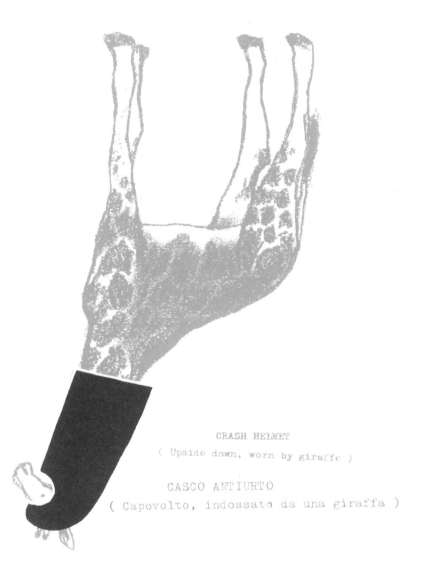

CRASH HELMET
(Upside down, worn by giraffe)

CASCO ANTIURTO
(Capovolto, indossato da una giraffa)

1–2
Pages from *A is for Rhinoceros*
(Edizioni Corraini, 2005).

Deckchairs with odd-shaped shadows

Sedie a sdraio con ombre dalla strana forma

3

3–5
Cover and spreads from
A Colouring Book for the Lazy
(Edizioni Corraini, 2006).
Russell's irreverent versions of
alphabet and counting books are
witty and sophisticated, designed
to be enjoyed by all age-groups.

Di solito il gatto abita nella carbonaia e l'orso polare vive nella bufera di neve, ma oggi hanno deciso di scambiarsi di posto.

Normally the cat lives in the coal cellar and the polar bear in the snow storm, but today they decided to swap.

4

Magpie Pie

5

Older children

Publishers' attitudes to the desirability or otherwise of
illustration for older age-groups vary greatly from country to
country. At worst, illustration can be seen as being relevant
only to the three- to seven-year-old age-group - the picturebook
as a stepping-stone to reading. Once basic literacy is achieved,
the image becomes superfluous. More enlightened cultures
recognize the role of illustration for all age-groups. In
France and Japan, for example, the *bande dessinée* or adult
comic is a well-established medium that is not regarded as in
any way less intellectually demanding than the word-based novel.
Traditionally, at least in the UK, there has been a wealth of
illustration for older children in the context of anthologies
or collections of stories, sometimes known as 'gift books' or
'treasuries'. These were particularly prevalent at the time of
what has become known as the 'Golden Age' of illustration, when
the work of artists such as Arthur Rackham and Howard Pyle was
lavishly reproduced in collectable editions of classic stories.
The role of illustration here is fundamentally different from
that of pictures in picturebooks. Here the text can exist
independently of the image and can be read and understood
perfectly well without pictorial support. The image augments
and embellishes the reader's experience.

In recent years, the use of illustration for older children has
declined somewhat, due, some feel, to what has been termed the
'Harry Potter effect' - the boom in fantasy novels (and their
spin-offs) leading to a perception that pictures are redundant.
Of course once the film of the book appears, the whole visual
aesthetic changes too, and film stills tend to become the order of
the day. There are those who feel that illustration generally can
interfere with the reader's personal visual imagination, taking
ownership of it and intruding on the experience. This should not
be the case. Imaginative illustration should act as a prompt or a
stimulus and can greatly enhance the aesthetic experience of the
book. Successful illustration of this kind depends on the
artist's empathy with and respect for the author's words.

In this section I have concentrated on books for older children
where the illustration has played a key role and where publishers
have bravely embraced illustration as a prominent element in the
story-telling process.

lisa evans

'Details influence me. Journeys and processes, subtle narratives and subplots. I like the merging of fact and fiction and the endless possibilities an image provides.' Lisa Evans studied illustration at the University of the West of England and went on to take her Masters in Children's Book Illustration at Cambridge School of Art, Anglia Ruskin University in England. *The Flower* (Child's Play, 2006) is Lisa's first picturebook. She says: 'It's a beautiful text written by John Light. It's about a boy on a mission to restore "soul" into the world. At least that's my take on it. It explores personal courage, determination and hope.' Set in a bleak future metropolis, the text is an ideal vehicle for the artist's dark, poetic vision. Characters have a haunted, lost feel and the words and pictures somehow appear to merge seamlessly. She works with acrylics on gesso and sometimes in pencil 'fluffed up' in Photoshop.

1

1–7
Title page and interior spreads from *The Flower* (written by John Light, Child's Play, 2006). Evans' rather theatrical illustrations perfectly complement John Light's thoughtful text. Limited colour reflects the dark, Orwellian nature of the early part of the book. Colour begins to creep in as the text conveys an increasing sense of hope.

Brigg lived in a small room in a big city.

2

Every day he walked through the city to work.

3

In an old part of the city he came to a junk shop . . .

. . . and there in the window was a dusty picture of some flowers.

4

At last he dried his eyes and set off to search for another packet of seeds.
After many weeks he came to the edge of the city where the dust heaps were.

5

On one of the heaps he saw the dead flower,
and all round it were new green shoots.
Here is another line tra la la.........hhmmmmmmmmmmmmm
I do hope this is going to be a good book. I hope it looks
real pretty on the book shelves.
Hmmmm heres another line. Tick tock. Did you know I
had a dream that I was in page seven of this book....

6

At last the plant flowered and Brigg
was overjoyed.

7

sara fanelli

Sara Fanelli is one of the most admired artists working in the field of children's books today. Her graphic work consistently pushes at the boundaries of what is considered visually 'appropriate' for children and she has spawned a plethora of imitators. She is passionate about books, and has worked with a number of publishers in the UK alongside her other work in editorial, design and advertising.

Originally from Florence, Italy, Sara studied at Camberwell School of Art and the Royal College of Art in London. At times it has seemed that the status of her work within the graphic art world is at odds with the inherent conservatism of the UK children's publishing market. She feels that this situation is beginning to improve and that high-quality books are now beginning to get past the marketing people and booksellers and onto the shelves. 'Because of the common language, the UK publishing industry has evolved with a built-in budget that involves selling large coeditions to the USA, so this has shaped the kinds of books that are published and promoted. In France for instance, where the language issue means there are not the same pressures, beautiful books can be published. Here in the UK, we still have a predominance of TV spin-offs and so on.'

Speaking about the ways that each of her books might evolve, Sara says, 'With *My Map Book* (Walker Books, 1995) I had been looking at Jean-Michel Basquait's work and I had always been interested in the narrative aspect of maps. These things came together. With *Dear Diary* (Walker Books, 2000) it was driven more by an interest in the aesthetic of stationery initially but gradually the narrative became increasingly important.' Among the various projects on which she is currently working is a 40-metre (130-ft) hanging for the Tate Britain Gallery in London.

1
A vignette illustration from *Pinocchio* (Carlo Collodi, translated by Emma Rose, Walker Books, 2004). Fanelli depicts herself as a child drawing Pinocchio.

2–3
Interior spreads from *Pinocchio*.

1

2

3

4

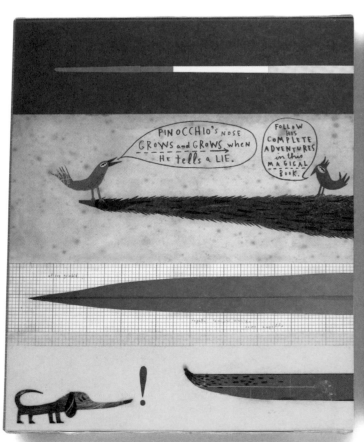
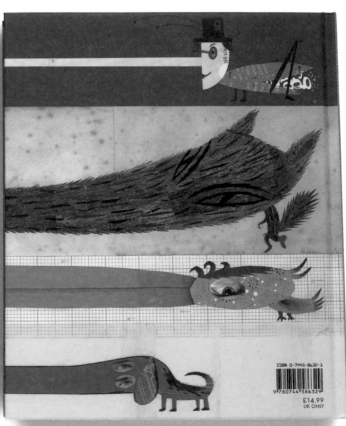

5

4–5
Front and back view of
Pinocchio. Fanelli's cover design
cleverly incorporates a slipcase
that elongates the eponymous
character's nose as the book is
drawn out.

6
Single-page illustration from
Pinocchio. Sara Fanelli uses
traditional cut-paper collage
interspersed with pen-and-ink
drawing to create her distinctive
illustrations.

6

pieter gaudesaboos

Speaking of his acclaimed book, *Roodlapje* ('Little Red Rag', Lannoo Publishing, 2003), Belgian artist Pieter Gaudesaboos says: 'Because the story felt so real (and my hand-drawn illustrations are bright and full of colour), I decided to use photography.' These haunting photo-illustrations brought the book nominations for awards and it has, he says, been 'surprisingly popular . . . particularly with art students'. Although often marketed among pre-reading picturebooks, the book is perhaps best seen as a picturebook for older readers. Gaudesaboos explains, 'Here in Belgium, you'll find two sorts of books. There are the traditional ones (classic children's stories about horses, dolphins, etc.), and then you have the "arty" picturebooks. These are made for children and adults and after more than ten years, there really is a market for this kind of artwork here in Belgium. I have done a few books for young children but I always find it a particular compliment if adults appreciate my work.'

Speaking to Marita Vermeulen in *Colouring Outside the Lines* (Flemish Literature Fund/Lannoo Publishing, 2006), the artist explains how *Roodlapje* evolved: '. . . I imagined a child's head as a house with lots and lots of rooms. All the rooms are different and you have to go through all of them in order to understand the child.'

Gaudesaboos studied Graphic Design for three years, followed by a further two years studying Photography. 'After that, I visited a few publishers to show them my portfolio and entertain them with a few ideas. They all seemed to be interested and told me to "create something" and then return. I had expected to be given a text. So I went back home and started to write a few things down, about a little girl who's so lonely she invents a world of her own.' Like Jeff Fisher (see page 88), he feels that the overall visual authorial role that he has as writer and graphic designer is important: 'As designer, I'm able to hold control of everything. I'm making my own layouts, I'm doing the illustrations and writing the text. When I start making a book, it's more than just the illustrations, it's the whole package.' In this context, he feels the word 'illustrator' is perhaps inappropriate. 'I think I'm more of a storyteller.'

1

1–4
Spreads from *Roodlapje* ('Little Red Rag', Lannoo, 2003). Pieter Gaudesaboos employs an unusual mix of photography, found imagery and heavily pixelated computer-games graphics to create this powerful, urban visual narrative.

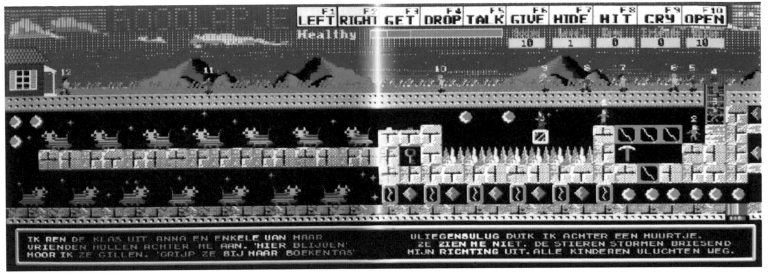

IK REN DE KLAS UIT. ANNA EN ENKELE VAN HAAR
VRIENDEN HOLLEN ACHTER ME AAN. 'HIER BLIJVEN'
HOOR IK ZE GILLEN. 'GRIJP ZE BIJ HAAR BOEKENTAS'

VLIEGENSVLUG DUIK IK ACHTER EEN MUURTJE.
ZE ZIEN ME NIET. DE STIEREN STORMEN BRIESEND
MIJN RICHTING UIT. ALLE KINDEREN VLUCHTEN WEG.

2

*** waarom verkoudjuw?
kunnen de stieren je wel verstaan? ***

'Geen idee' zei Lapje.
'k heb 't altijd zo geweten.
Misschien was 't vroeger anders
maar dat ben ik vergeten.

Ik vertel ze over Pees,
ruinpieren, vis en vossen.
Over kleine meisjes, heel alleen,
verdwaald in grote bossen.

Maar waarom, nee dat weet ik niet
het was zo van in 't begin.
En nu terug veranderen,
dat heeft toch echt geen zin.

VRAAGJE

3

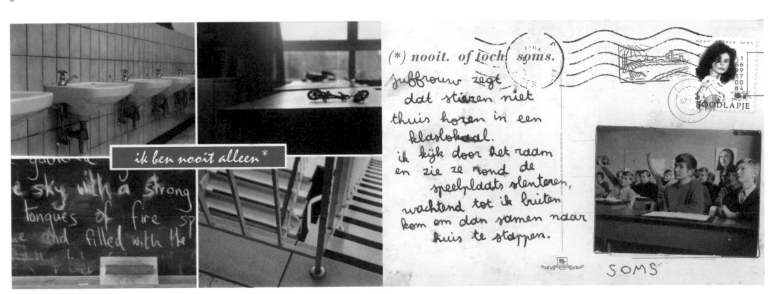

ik ben nooit alleen *

e sky with a strong
tongues of fire sp
e and filled with the

(*) nooit. of toch soms.

Juffrouw zegt
dat stieren niet
thuis horen in een
klaslokaal.
ik kijk door het raam
en zie ze rond de
speelplaats slenteren,
wachtend tot ik buiten
kom om dan samen naar
huis te stappen.

RODLAPJE

SOMS

4

david hughes

Often regarded as the 'enfant terrible' of illustration, David Hughes has been an influential presence in the graphic arts for nearly three decades, having begun his working life in TV graphics. His virtuoso draughtsmanship with its distinctively spiky edge has graced the pages of numerous magazines and newspapers around the world, as well as set designs for national television productions. Uncompromisingly hard-hitting and, at times, grotesque in his editorial work, Hughes may not seem the most likely children's book illustrator-author. He has, however, produced many picturebooks, some of them under his own name, others under his children's book pseudonym, Sandy Turner, a name that came about in curious circumstances: 'I was having a particularly difficult time with an editorial client in America,' he told me. 'The illustration was being repeatedly sent back to me for changes. There were so many changes made that I became completely disillusioned with the job and felt it was no longer my work. I wanted to disown it. I told them they could publish if they used a different name. I quickly came up with the blandest, most gender-neutral name I could think of - Sandy Turner. Shortly afterwards, an American literary agent called, having seen the image, asking to speak to Sandy Turner and offering a picturebook. So I was stuck with the name.' Under this name, David has authored and illustrated a number of highly inventive picturebooks in recent years.

Victor Hugo's *The Hunchback of Notre-Dame* (translated and adapted by Jan Needle, 2006) was commissioned by Walker Books for their classics series. Hughes feels that he 'found himself' again with this book, 'a sort of "relaunching" of David Hughes' is how he describes it. He threw himself into this commission with typical dedication, visiting Paris to research the book. 'I had to go to Notre Dame,' he says - 'I wanted to really enjoy this book. Once I got over my initial reluctance to take it on, I threw myself into it. I'd had the text for six months before I did anything. I was sent a dummy book and worked directly into it. It was like carrying a laptop around, an old-fashioned version.' Working with the designer Liz Wood, he ended up with 140 images, instead of the planned 40. David Hughes's evident pride in this book is particularly meaningful given his highly self-critical nature.

1

2

3

1–3
Cover and interior spreads from *Cool Cat, Hot Dog* (Atheneum, 2005). Produced under Hughes' erstwhile children's book pseudonym, Sandy Turner.

4
Cover for *The Hunchback of Notre-Dame* (translated by Jan Needle, Walker Books, 2006).

4

5

5–6
Double-page spreads from
The Hunchback of Notre-Dame.
Hughes' virtuoso
draughtsmanship and graphic
flair, along with Walker Books'
Liz Woods' excellent design
make this book a triumph of
production.

Around her all eyes were fixed, all mouths gaping open; and, in truth, dancing like that to the beating of a tambourine held above her head in her pure, shapely arms, slim, neat and lively as a wasp, with her golden bodice and twirling skirt, her bare shoulders, her slender legs uncovered now and then, her coal-black hair and eyes of fire, she was a supernatural beauty.

Truly, thought Gringoire, it is a creature of the flames, it is a nymph, a goddess, a bacchante!

Then one of the braids that held her hair came loose, and a small brass coin fell out of it and clattered to the ground.

"Oh, no," said Gringoire, all illusion shattered. "It's just a gypsy."

However disenchanted Pierre might be, however, the scene still held a certain magic. Among the hordes of faces made crimson by the fire's glow, one in particular seemed held in fascination by the dancing girl. It was a man's face, dark, calm and sombre. His clothes were hidden by the crowd, but – although he looked only thirty-five or so – he was almost bald, with only tufts of grey, his high, broad forehead already lined. But in his deepset eyes there shined an extraordinary youthfulness, an ardent life force, passion. He never took them from the gypsy girl, and as the wild young creature danced and vaulted to the joy of everyone, he became more sombre, more absorbed. From time to time a smile and a sigh would come together to his lips; but the smile was always sadder than the sigh.

At last the young girl, out of breath, stopped dancing, and the people clapped her, full of shared pleasure.

"Djali!" she said.

maurizio quarello

Maurizio Quarello's painterly, atmospheric imagery draws on classical influences: the Flemish painters Pieter Bruegel, Hieronymus Bosch and Jan van Eyck; Germans Matthias Grünewald and Albrecht Dürer; and of course the Italian Renaissance. 'But I'm also inspired by George Grosz, Edward Hopper, Ernst Ludwig Kirchner, Frantisek Skala, Jan Svankmajer and many others. I am also a great fan of cinema, especially older movies with amazing atmosphere and design. I try to illustrate my books like a movie. I decided to become an illustrator because I love figurative painting. I love books, all kinds of books, not just those for children. I enjoy the work of the old masters and hope to do some good by following in those traditions.'

Born in Italy, Quarello studied Graphic Advertising, Architecture and Illustration in Turin. He has studied under Jindra Capek and Linda Wolfsburger. Quarello found it hard to get started in the world of illustration: 'My first published work came after I won an illustration competition in Italy. I went on to illustrate a story written entirely by children. I wasn't sure that my work was right for children. Now I know that they love it - they seem to like scary stories and scary images, just like me. I am happy that a jury of children has voted my *Babau Cerca Casa* the best Italian book of 2006.' Speaking about his methods and approaches he says, 'I don't have a "right way" to illustrate, I just try to see things as I would as a child.' As an established and acclaimed artist he is now able to create 'prototypes' of visual ideas and stories to offer to publishers and to collaborate with young writers. Considering the relationship between 'art' and illustration, he observes, 'You may not have total creative freedom as a children's book illustrator. The text, of course, may be chosen by the publisher. There is the question of commerce. It is not necessarily possible to express everything that I would like, but I think it is an important challenge for an artist to interpret within limitations. Limitations are good for the personal creative progress of an artist.'

1

Marizul, asustada, se refugió tras el genio.

– ¿Quién es?

– **La recolectora de sueños.**
Cuando terminas un sueño,
se lo embolsa y no lo suelta nunca más.

– **Imposible. Una vez tuve un sueño**
que ya había soñado…

– **Seguro que no.**
En el más escondido rincón de tu sueño
habría algo distinto.
Además, aunque te resultasen idénticos,
en el segundo estaba el recuerdo del primero.

– **¿Guarda también los sueños de los perritos?**

– **Y los de los caballos,**
de los gatos y hasta de los pájaros,
que siempre son sueños de volar
o de no poder volar.

– **¿Es buena o mala?** -preguntó Marizul
mientras la anciana seguía su camino.

– **No es buena, ni mala, ni nada**
-rió el genio como loco.

2

Sentada en el sillón, nunca Marizul había visto
tantos objetos juntos en desuso:
sillas, percheros, cañones, triciclos,
sombreros, relojes, guantes, sombrillas…
se apilaban aquí y allá,
casi sin dejar ver ni cielo ni tierra.

Sobre una pila de trastos,
un genio escarlata sonreía.

– **¿Dónde estoy?**

– **En la tierra de lo que se perdió**
y jamás se encontró -contestó el genio.

– **¿Tristana está aquí?**
-preguntó Marizul, esperanzada,
pensando en la muñeca que había perdido
en un paseo por el campo.

– **Tu muñeca no llegó aquí**
porque la encontró una niña campesina.
Le ha hecho cinco vestidos nuevos
y, como llevaba su nombre bordado,
le sigue llamando Tristana.

3

– ¿Hay también una Marizul de orejas largas?

– Y una de ojos verdes,
otra de trenzas rubias…

– ¡Grande ha de ser esta tierra!

– Tanto como para que quepa
todo lo que pudo ser y no fue
-dijo el hada, con entusiasmo.

4

4
A double-page spread illustration
from *Marizul…*.

5
'Ork', an unpublished illustration,
exhibited at the exhibition 'Italian
Illustrators Celebrate the Grimm
Brothers', Bologna, 2006.

5

margarita sada

Mexican artist Margarita Sada studied design at the National Institute of Fine Arts in Mexico City, a school where she says the emphasis was on links between design and professional fine arts execution. 'Afterwards I took a painting MA at San Carlos Academy - National University of Mexico Fine Arts School, where I actually learned how to paint. I believe that handling the tools of design on one side and painting on the other has been the cornerstone in achieving skills for conceptual and technical freedom in working with texts.'

Sada works mainly within the field of children's books but also illustrates for adults on cultural affairs: 'Outside of these I use my spare time to paint and develop my own projects.' The book, *La Enfermedad del Beso* ('The Kissing Disease', written by Maria Emilia Beyer Ruiz, Castillo, 2006) deals with a virus transmitted through kissing. Clearly a difficult subject to deal with visually, Sada found the project challenging but rewarding: 'For obvious reasons, the book is mostly aimed at adolescents. Although the text has a formal format, illustrating this book was fun for me because it made me remember such an odious stage of my life and because it gave me the chance to work on many different characters. Some of my friends served as models, without having a clue. And finally, of course, who doesn't care about kisses?' These illustrations manage to strike just the right visual tone for the subject - playful yet serious.

Since *La Enfermedad del Beso*, she has illustrated *De Principios y Princesas* ('On Principles and Princesses', Castillo, 2006), which Sada describes as 'A sort of art catalogue of an exhibition dedicated to illusory nobles throughout history. The stories are real but not necessarily true to particular names or events. It's an amusing way to educate children on biography and to develop an interest in history.'

1

1–3
Images from *La Enfermedad del Beso* ('The Kissing Disease', written by Maria Emilia Beyer Ruiz, Castillo, 2006). Sada treats a difficult subject with sensitivity and humour.

2

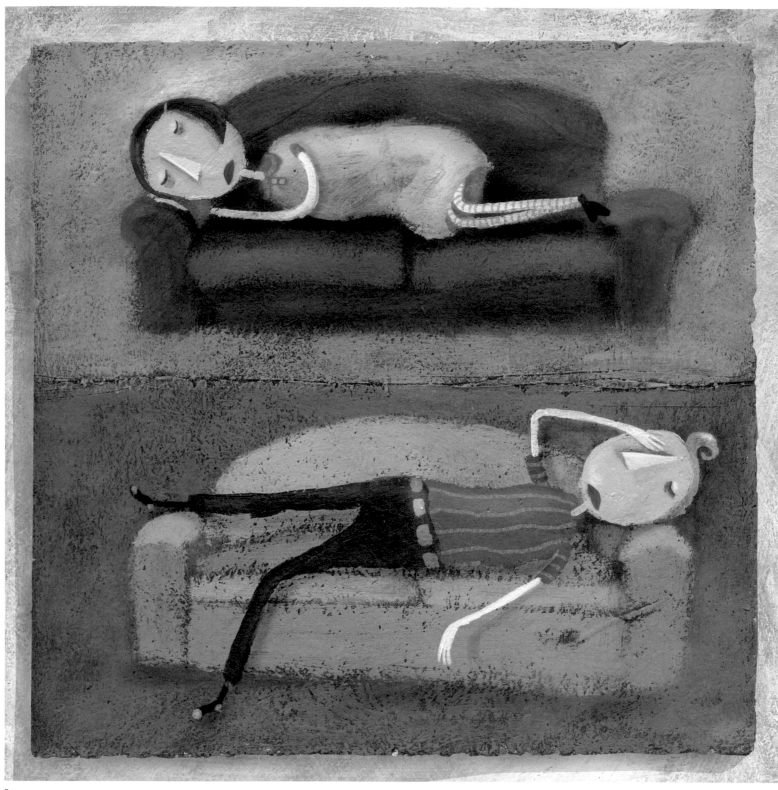

3

4
Illustrations from *De Principios y Princesas* ('On Principles and Princesses', Castillo, 2006). Here Sada fuses her own visual motifs with the familiar imagery of Renaissance Italy.

isabelle vandenabeele

In *Colouring Outside the Lines* (Flemish Literature Fund/ Lannoo Publishing, 2006), Marita Vermeulen writes about Vandenabeele's illustrations to *Rood Rood Roodkapje* ('Little Red Riding Hood', written by Edward van de Vendel, De Eenhoorn, 2003): 'For anyone who likes innocent little children being saved by strong hunters, entering these pictures is undoubtedly somewhat of a challenge.' Vandenabeele's raw, uncompromising woodcut illustrations are certainly not of the fluffy-bunny school of children's book illustration. Working with limited colour, bold, harsh shapes and often keeping her characters' features away from centre-stage, she breaks many of the supposed rules of the game.

Isabelle Vandenabeele studied at art school in her home country of Belgium from 1990 to 1997, initially Graphic Design but later being able to concentrate on Printmaking: 'I learned different processes - lithography, etching, woodcut . . . It was a free, artistic environment and these techniques inspired me. I was able to draw a lot and this became figurative, narrative. It evolved into what they call illustration.' Speaking of her approach to her work, she goes on, 'I'm not always very good at expressing myself in words. I prefer to speak by making images. I'm very inspired by things around me - little things that make everything different. I like to put these situations and nuances into my drawings. The main "subject" of a story is sometimes less important, it's just a reason to tell of a lot of other things.' On influences, she says that as a student she was interested in an eclectic mix of artists including Henri 'Le Douanier' Rousseau, Tamara De Lempicka, Jean-Auguste-Dominique Ingres and Richard Diebenkorn as well as illustrators such as Jacques de Loustal, Jean-Claude Götting, Lorenzo Mattotti and Ana Juan.

The story of the publication of *Rood Rood Roodkapje* is an interesting example of modern visual authorship, and of personal creative experimentation going on to reach a wider audience in the form of a mass-produced book. The artist had made a number of experimental woodcuts inspired by the story with an idea about possibly making an artists' book (that is, employing the medium of the book to produce an original work of art, usually produced as one-of-a-kind or in small edition multiples). However, at an exhibition of the prints, her publisher, De Eenhoorn, suggested a children's book. 'They suggested Edward van de Vendel as the writer. Edward wrote the story from looking at the prints. We never had contact.' After this project, she was keen to experiment technically, and on the next book, *Mijn Schaduw en Ik* ('My Shadow and Me', written by Pieter van Oudheusden, De Eenhoorn, 2005), she printed each colour separately then scanned and reassembled them in Photoshop. They were then printed by offset litho, one colour over the other. The subtle effects of shadow on colour are brilliantly portrayed through this method.

1

From *Mijn Schaduw en Ik* ('My Shadow and Me', written by Pieter van Oudheusden, De Eenhorn, 2005). Vandenabeele's raw, robust woodcut illustrations, rendered in strong colours, are laden with powerful narrative tension.

2–3
Spreads from *Een Griezelmeisje* ('A Horrorgirl', written by Edward van den Vendel, De Eenhorn, 2006).

2

3

4

From *Mijn Schaduw en Ik.*

noemí villamuza

The sensual, lyrical drawings of Spanish artist Noemí Villamuza comfortably combine old and new technology through the use of pencil and flat digital colour in, for example, *Me Gusta* (written by Javier Sobrino, Kókinos, 2002), or pencil and photo collage in *Libro de Nanas* (selected by Herrín Hidalgo, Media Vaca, 2004).

Villamuza was born in Palencia, Spain, in 1971 and studied Fine Arts in Salamanca. She has been dedicating herself to the art of illustrating for children for some eight or nine years now. She now lives and works in Barcelona. *Me Gusta* ('I Like') explores the everyday experiences of the senses, the wind on the face, the sight of the sun setting, the 'cri-cri' sound of crickets. The artist's compositions are at the same time simple but ambitious; economical but powerful in their use of picture space and viewpoint. Villamuza brings something new to the writer's words on each spread, little pictorial asides or visual counterpoints that are the mark of an artist with real sensitivity to the written word. In *Libro de Nanas* ('Book of Lullabies') Villamuza chooses to work entirely in black and white, her subtly textured pencil drawings sometimes boldly and strikingly coexisting with old engravings of objects from advertising manuals. She speaks of night-time being a time when the eyes take a rest from colour. She says that, as a child, she feared the dark because of the number of things she imagined existed out of sight. Now that she is grown up, she continues to be scared because she can imagine even more things.

1

1
Cover for *Libro de Nanas* ('Book of Lullabies', various contributing authors, Media Vaca, 2004).

2–3
Double-page spreads from *Me Gusta* ('I Like', written by Javier Sobrino, Kókinos, 2002).

4–7 (overleaf)
Spreads from *Libro de Nanas*. Bold pencil drawings are mixed with collaged engraved objects to create striking monochrome page designs.

Me gusta vivir...
con el aire fresco en la cara
y con tus risas detrás de mi.

2

3

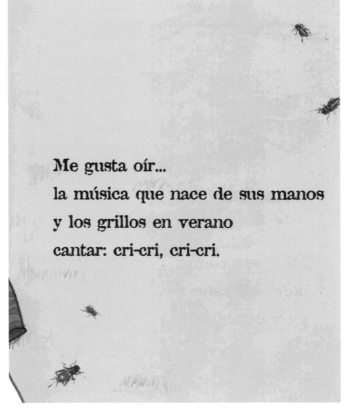

Me gusta oír...
la música que nace de sus manos
y los grillos en verano
cantar: cri-cri, cri-cri.

4

NANA DEL NIÑO MALO

PABLO GUERRERO

El niño malo dijo:
«Me gusta el Che»
y ha dado a su abuelita
un puntapié.

Ha roto siete vasos,
tres cacerolas
y llamó a Doña Carmen
Vieja Cotorra

Ea la nana, ea.

El niño malo tiene
en la cocina
amordazado al Coco
sobre una silla.

Pajareando anda
el niño malo
y ha pedido una novia
a los Reyes Magos

Ea la nana, ea.

¿Qué será de mayor
nuestro angelito?
Su padre que Teniente,
su madre Obispo.

El abuelo Ingeniero,
la abuelita Abogado.
Y el niño malo dijo:
«Quiero ser Vago».

Ea la nana, ea.

32

33

5

YO NO TENGO SOLEDAD

GABRIELA MISTRAL

Es la noche desamparo
de las sierras hasta el mar.
Pero yo, la que te mece,
¡yo no tengo soledad!

Es el cielo desamparo
si la luna cae al mar.
Pero yo, la que te estrecha,
¡yo no tengo soledad!

Es el mundo desamparo
y la carne triste va.
Pero yo, la que te oprime,
¡yo no tengo soledad!

6

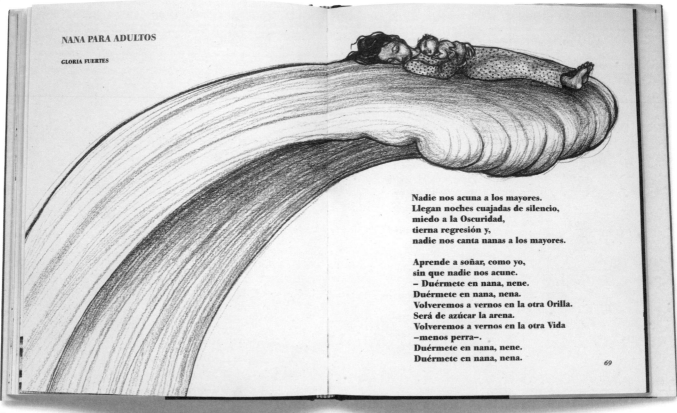

NANA PARA ADULTOS

GLORIA FUERTES

Nadie nos acuna a los mayores.
Llegan noches cuajadas de silencio,
miedo a la Oscuridad,
tierna regresión y,
nadie nos canta nanas a los mayores.

Aprende a soñar, como yo,
sin que nadie nos acune.
– Duérmete en nana, nene.
Duérmete en nana, nena.
Volveremos a vernos en la otra Orilla.
Será de azúcar la arena.
Volveremos a vernos en la otra Vida
—menos perra–.
Duérmete en nana, nene.
Duérmete en nana, nena.

69

7

Non-fiction

The demands placed on the artist when visualizing and explaining factual information can be very different from those faced in the context of narrative fiction. Often the need to cram information into small areas of space can limit the scope for real creative invention. There are a number of artists who excel in the traditional methods of factual illustration and who also manage to bring individuality and beauty to their work. The elaborate cutaway illustrations of Stephen Biesty, for example, immediately spring to mind, his enormous knowledge and depth of scrupulous research being distilled into sumptuously designed visual explanations of the workings of ocean liners, interior details of medieval castles or the streets and buildings of ancient Rome. Steve Noon's meticulously depicted sequential representations of places as they evolve and change through time sit in the great tradition of non-fiction illustration and are executed with a skill and painterly vision that is now perhaps something of a rarity.

Working within non-fiction illustration requires a combination of artistic vision and scientific curiosity. Currently, the use of humour appears to dominate the delivery of history and geography in publishing, as evidenced by highly popular series such as the Terry Deary/Martin Brown 'Horrible Histories'. The design of visual non-fiction information in children's books is being addressed in increasingly inventive ways. Children are now introduced to science, the humanities, art, politics, popular culture and more through sophisticated yet entertaining book concepts and formats. Often, narrative threads and characters are woven into an idea to capture and hold the attention of a young audience, an advanced version perhaps of Bishop Comenius's notion 350 years ago that pictures could lighten the tedium of learning Latin. Sometimes such devices can appear contrived or 'gimmicky' but often they are genuinely original and effective in engaging children in subjects in which they would not otherwise be consciously interested.

The artists whose work is featured in the non-fiction section are not, by and large, non-fiction 'specialists'. They are artists and designers who work across the graphic arts and who I feel have brought something fresh to this particular field of children's book publishing. Many of them can be seen to represent the growing number of artists and designers who are bringing their own authorial ideas to the world of children's book publishing as the practice of illustration continues to move away from its traditional status as subservient to the written word.

serge bloch

Serge Bloch is, quite simply, a brilliant visual communicator. His playful, thoughtful graphic work appears regularly not just in books for children, but in such august publications as *The New York Times*, the *Boston Globe*, *The Washington Post*, *Wall Street Journal*, *Los Angeles Times* and the *Chicago Tribune*. In 2005, he was awarded a gold medal at the American Society of Illustrators' 47th Exhibition. Educated at the School of Decorative Arts, Strasbourg, France, Bloch has illustrated over two hundred books in his native France, where he is also art director for a leading publisher of books and magazines for children. He is the creator of *Sansom*, 'the smallest of big heroes', *Toto's Jokes* and *Max and Lili*, who are extremely popular in France, Switzerland and Canada. 'For me,' he says, 'working for children or adults, on books, newspapers or advertisements, it's the same thing - amusing me to amuse future readers. I am not a narrator, I do not tell tales. I just draw things, people, moments . . . that I have taken in.'

Bloch has many thoughts to share on the subject of illustration and drawing. He says, for instance: 'Drawing well takes a great deal of observation, a moderate amount of instruction (three years at art school should do) and a lifetime of dis-instruction. To create, you need to stay in childhood. Children are born creators. Creativity is a normal language for them. As adults, we lose a lot of our gifts.' Humour is an essential component of his graphic work, subtle and understated, making its point '*par un sourire plus que le rire* (with a smile rather than a laugh)'. He describes humour as 'a fabulous means of communication'. The idea is paramount: 'No idea,' he explains, 'no drawing. "Style" is not my cup of tea . . . it slows the idea down. It keeps the idea from reaching the person watching for it.'

'I enjoy, and try to make, humorous work; a minor, modest art-form. No relation to Art with a capital A. But I am sure that one day someone will build a second MoMA - the Museum of Modest Art - much smaller than the other one, where you will be able to admire the work of humorist illustrators from Charles Addams to William Steig, and all the others, well known and not so well known.'

1

1–6
Cover, endpapers and interior illustrations for *L'Ennemi* ('The Enemy', written by Davide Cali, Sarbacane, 2007). Bloch's elegant graphic wit is in the great tradition of artists such as Ronald Searle and André Francois. Here he illustrates an ironic exploration of the propaganda of war.

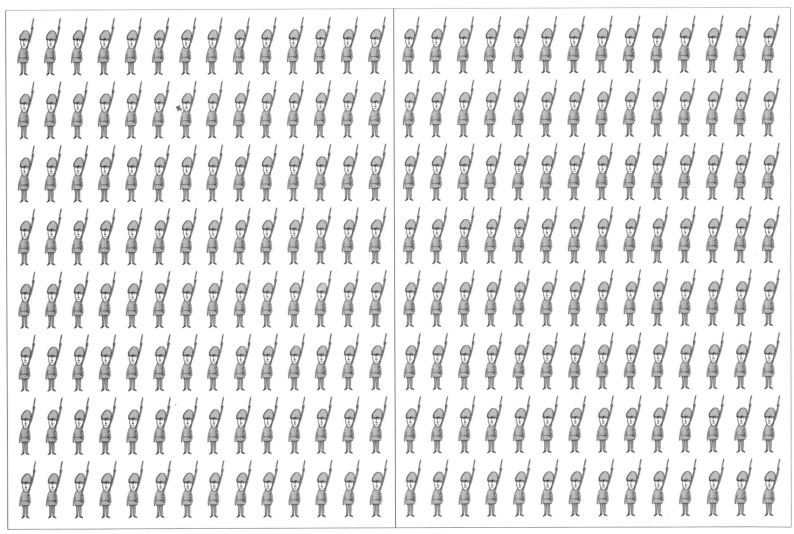

2

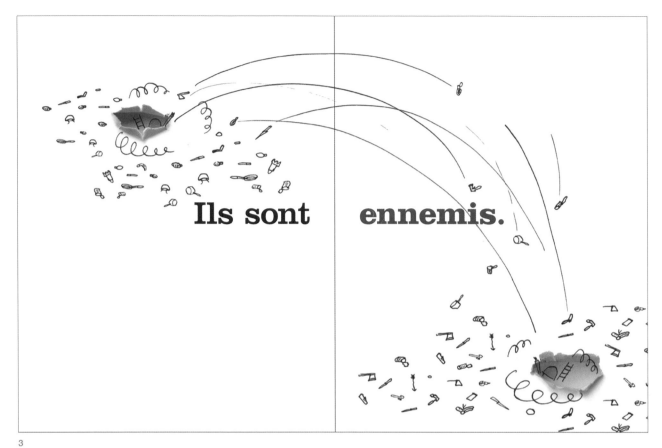

Ils sont ennemis.

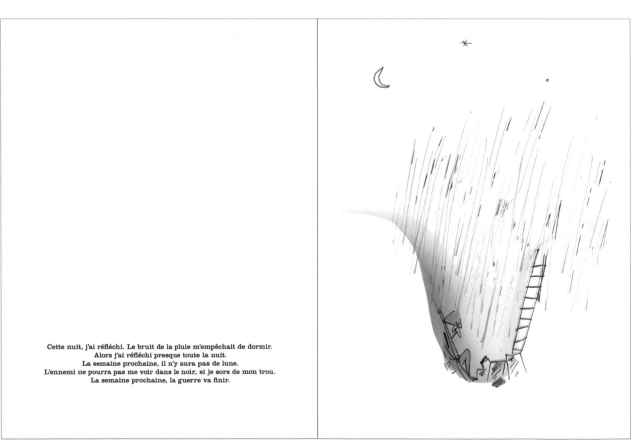

Cette nuit, j'ai réfléchi. Le bruit de la pluie m'empêchait de dormir.
Alors j'ai réfléchi presque toute la nuit.
La semaine prochaine, il n'y aura pas de lune.
L'ennemi ne pourra pas me voir dans le noir, si je sors de mon trou.
La semaine prochaine, la guerre va finir.

Même si j'ai faim, j'attends.
J'attends que ce soit l'ennemi qui allume son feu
parce que si j'allumais le mien,
il pourrait en profiter pour s'approcher, et me tuer.

Mais quelquefois, j'ai tellement faim
que j'allume mon feu le premier.
Aussitôt, l'ennemi allume son feu.

Le premier jour de guerre, il y a longtemps,
ils nous ont donné un fusil et un manuel.

Le manuel dit tout sur l'ennemi :
il dit qu'il faut le tuer avant qu'il ne nous tue,
parce qu'il est cruel et impitoyable.
S'il nous tue, il exterminera nos familles.
Mais il ne sera pas satisfait pour autant.
Il tuera les chiens et puis tous les animaux,
il brûlera les bois, il empoisonnera l'eau.
L'ennemi n'est pas un être humain.

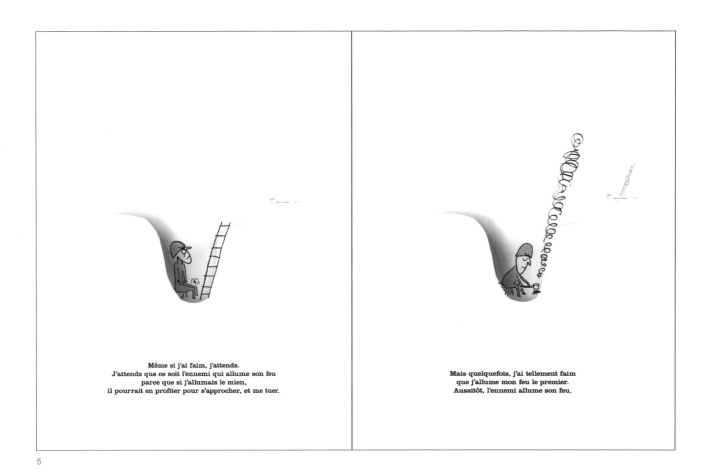

jason ford

Perhaps best known for his instantly recognizable work in editorial illustration over the last 20 or so years, Jason Ford has recently contributed to children's publishing across a variety of areas, particularly book covers for early teens and notably his series of cover designs for the titles of Enid Blyton for Egmont Books. Ford was brought up in Bath in the west of England and went on to study Graphic Design at Brighton Polytechnic (now the University of Brighton). 'Illustration and design were separate pathways, but I enjoyed graphic design too. I was very much into comic culture - Tintin, Asterix, Marvel Comics and so on. Chris McEwen was an influential tutor. We shared an interest in things like Westerns, 1950s sci-fi, film noir, Disney.' The retro, pulp-fiction aesthetic of Ford's illustration is created using a hand-painted line and adding digital colour: 'I only went over to digital about six years ago. I used to spend hours mixing paint and applying flat colour without the brush strokes being visible. I felt like I was cheating once I became digital.'

Art Auction Mystery (written by Anna Nilsen, Kingfisher, 2005) is the third in a series of books by this author that introduce children to the great works of art from museums around the world by placing the paintings in a narrative detective-fiction context. Ford's illustrations are used here to great effect, creating an appropriate, slightly ironic detective fiction feel. The particular challenge for the artist here was to work with various elements that needed to be dropped into the images, usually photographs of actual paintings, in frames or on the pages of an illustration of a book: 'It was quite complicated to do. I had to leave a lot of space for other elements and consider their impact on the composition.'

1
From *Art Auction Mystery* (written by Anna Nilsen, Kingfisher, 2005).

2
Ford needed to plan carefully to integrate photographic reproductions of fine art images with his artwork.

1

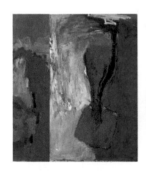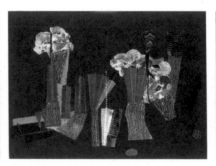

THE GREAT ART AUCTION
CATALOGUE

2

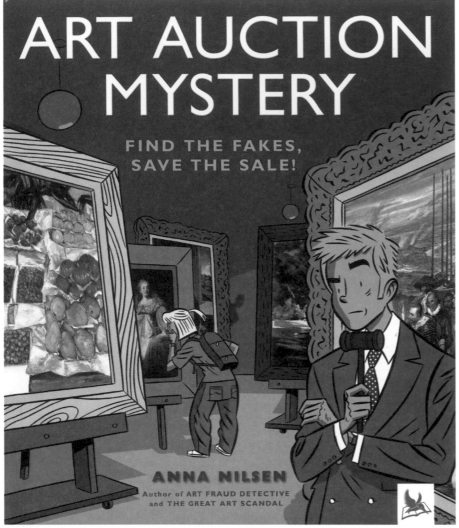

3–5
Cover and further interior
illustrations from *Art Auction
Mystery.*

3

4

THE CALL TO POLICE

neal
layton

As a schoolboy, Neal Layton found it hard to choose between art and science when looking at higher education. He was accepted at university to study for a science degree: 'I didn't do art at school. I chose French instead. I thought it would be more useful. I was good at maths. I think my maths teacher was disappointed that I didn't pursue the subject. He thought I was crazy to go to art school. He said I was a born mathematician. But I had begun visiting galleries and become increasingly interested in art. I thought: "this is more me". I don't think science and art are actually a million miles apart, though.' He enrolled on an Art Foundation course and found it a big culture shock: 'I hadn't really done any drawing before. I was given a sheet of A1 paper to draw on. It was a real learning curve.' He went on to study Graphic Design at the University of Northumbria in Newcastle and then took an MA at Central Saint Martins in London. Between the two courses he began to think more about children's books: 'I had entered the Macmillan Prize for Children's Picturebook Illustration while at Newcastle, but hadn't been accepted.' At CSM he worked purposely within the area of children's books, developing a project that examined the extent to which he could express himself artistically within this field. He says: 'Before joining the MA I had taken advice from the Association of Illustrators who had pointed out that my work showed a clear interest in character and in word-image relationships. I hadn't really been conscious of this, but my sketchbooks have always been filled with words as well as pictures.' This flair for writing, coupled with a keen interest in design has led to a distinctive series of picturebooks that are instantly recognizable by their slightly anarchic tone; Layton's wiry, scribbly line communicating with a direct, child-like charm.

The Story of Everything (Hodder, 2006) is 'an extremely brief history of the universe and you, told in 12 *and a bit* pages.' This highly entertaining introduction to life on earth wraps knowledge in fun, humour and play and can be enjoyed by all ages. The idea had been gestating for a while and took four years to complete. 'Anne McNeil at Hodder had suggested that I try to do something on human evolution. I went away and started drawing and thinking. I kept working further backwards and ending up with the Big Bang. So it grew into a story of everything. Fortunately, they liked it.'

Poo: A Natural History of the Unmentionable (written by Nicola Davies, Walker, 2005) was a commission that came about through Layton's fondness for hand-made, limited-edition photocopied books, something that he has always enjoyed making: 'We had such fun with it that we kept thinking "Are they really going to publish this?"'

1

1–4
Cover and interior spreads from
Poo: A Natural History of the Unmentionable (written by Nicola Davies, Walker Books, 2005).

A TOUR OF POO

Faeces can be so distinctive it's possible to identify an animal species just from its poo! Every animal has its own special sort of poo, so this is just a small sample of a huge variety of different poos (some were just too big or runny to fit on the page).

8

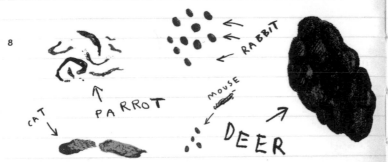

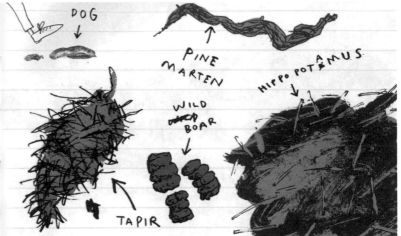

RAINBOW POOS

The one thing that doesn't seem to vary much between different sorts of poo is colour. Most are brownish or blackish. One reason for this is that mixing all the different colours in food is like mixing all the colours in a paint box – you get a kind of dark, yucky colour. Another reason is that when a body digests food it breaks down some of the colours it contained, leaving it dull and greyish. When this is added to the dark brown remains of dead blood cells chucked out by the body, hey presto you get the familiar poo-brown! Bird faeces are usually the typical dark-yuck colour too. But their droppings are splodged with white, because their white and pasty urine leaves their body through the same hole as their poo.

19

Sometimes an animal may eat so much of a brightly coloured food that the colour gets through to the poo (as anyone who's eaten beetroot soup will know!). Birds feasting on berries in the autumn can have droppings that look like sugar candy – pink or mauve from the berries, and striped with white. Blue whales, too, can have tinted faeces. When they feed on pink shrimps – swallowing a tonne in a single mouthful – they do huge pink poos that look like giant blobs of strawberry ice cream breaking up in the water.

BLUE-WHALE POO

3

POO DETECTIVES

Seeds are made extra strong to survive chewing and digestion, and there are other hard parts of food, such as bones or shells, that pop out in the poo as good as new. These can be useful if you want to know what an animal eats, especially if you can't watch it feeding.

Sperm whales hunt in the deepest water, up to 2,500 metres below the surface, where it is always cold and dark. At this depth the water pressure would crush a human like an ant, so no one can follow a sperm whale to see what it eats. But just before a sperm whale dives from the surface to these mysterious depths, it defecates and, if a whale scientist is quick, the poo can be scooped up in a net. The hard parts in the sperm whale's poo are horny jaws and teeth belonging to squid and sharks. By looking at them carefully, scientists now know that sperm whales can eat big sharks, and squid up to twenty metres long.

51

4

günter mattei

Winner of the Bologna Children's Book Fair Ragazzi Award (non-fiction) in 2006, Günter Mattei brings his highly original and eclectic approach to image-making to the world of children's books. Mattei has enjoyed a rich and varied creative career so far. He began by studying Window Display and then studied Graphic Design and Illustration at the Munich Graphic Design Centre in Germany. To fund his studies he worked part-time as a '*schriftenmaler*' - a poster artist: 'I did big signs and billboards and maybe learned more of value to my future work than I did at college.' On leaving art school, he went into partnership with his illustration teacher. Over the following years he worked for a wide range of clients in advertising and publishing.

Reflecting on his education and the evolution of his working methods, Mattei says that he realized at a very early age that 'drawing and visualizing things would be the best way to transport my ideas. I did study some techniques and I had a good teacher, but the way I work now is a result of very personal experiments and experiences. And these are difficult to teach or learn! When I was younger I had fun working in various "styles" or techniques and, at one stage, in order to be able to continue to do this professionally, I used three pseudonyms. Some clients didn't like that but I didn't care. The idea of being pigeonholed in a particular style was a horror to me. I felt it would take away my artistic freedom and future. Now, I don't have this problem!'

Mattei talks of three important strands to his work today, which he loosely categorizes as 'children, lifestyle and animals'. More specifically, these refer to his work with Schauburg-Theater der Jugend (the only communal theatre for young people in Germany), his design work for the chain of Schumann's Bars and, finally, his work with Munich Zoo, including his award-winning children's books in collaboration with Henning Wiesner, director of the zoo. 'The method or technique in these illustrations grew from the presentation boards I originally designed for the zoo, though it perhaps goes further back to my work as a poster artist. It's a way of working that comes primarily from technical needs but it became very popular and well known here in Munich and Bavaria. We won several awards. So it seemed natural to work in this way for *Müssen Tiere Zähne Putzen?* ('Do Animals Have to Clean their Teeth?', Hanser Verlag, 2005).'

Speaking about his relative interest in the areas of fiction or non-fiction, the artist says it's not an issue. 'It's a question of whether the theme touches me somehow. Is it important socially or to my artistic development? Will I have fun with it? One of the things I like most about being a designer-illustrator is the way I can be an actor and play different characters and make different rules. I don't think too much about the age range of the audience. Of course I try to consider whom I want to reach with my ideas. With the youth theatre I am working for people from ages four to eighty. I'm often surprised by what children can understand, but I don't want to think about it too much. I'd rather trust my gut feeling!'

1

1–2
From *Müssen Tiere Zähne Putzen?* ('Do Animals have to Clean their Teeth?', Hanser Verlag, 2005)

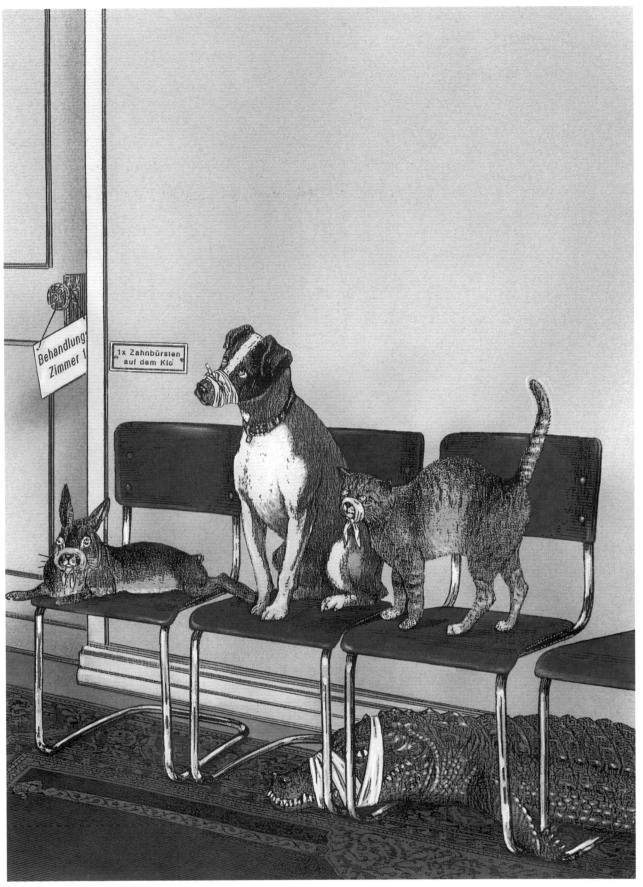

2

3–4

From *Das Große Buch der Tiere*
('The Large Book of Animals',
written by Henning Wiesner,
Hanser, 2005).

Ringelschwänzige Duftbotschaften

Die fuchsgesichtigen Kattas von Madagaskar sind überwiegend tagaktive Bodenbewohner, die in kleineren Trupps bis zu 20 Tieren auf Nahrungssuche gehen. In diesen kleinen Rudeln überwiegen zahlenmäßig die Männchen, während die weiblichen Tiere untereinander unverträglicher sind und vor allem während der Paarungssaison einander aus dem Trupp herauszubeißen versuchen. Ein derart unterlegenes Weibchen wird dann auch von den Männchen nicht mehr geduldet und gemeinsam vertrieben. Um ein hitziges Weibchen konnten wir zwischen den Männchen meist unblutige Auseinandersetzungen beobachten, nach deren Ende sich das Weibchen von allen daran beteiligten Männchen decken lässt.

Bei der Innengestaltung von Katta-Anlagen wird man diesem Verhalten insofern Rechnung tragen, als durch eine Vielzahl von Bäumen und Ästen der Raum von den Tieren optimal dreidimensional genutzt werden kann. So hat jedes der Tiere nicht nur einen eigenen Sitzplatz, sondern man kann sich auch bei Streitigkeiten „aus den Augen gehen". In den Ruhephasen nach der Nahrungsaufnahme finden sich die verschiedenen Familienmitglieder der Gruppe zur gegenseitigen Fellpflege oder aber zum „Kontaktschlafen" zusammen. Die so ruhenden Familien werden von fremden Kattas gemieden, vorwitzige Eindringlinge gemeinsam verjagt.

Zur Revierabgrenzung sowie zur Demonstration der individuellen Duftnote, die den Rangordnungsplatz des Tieres in der Gruppe signalisiert, markieren die Kattas mit speziellen, um den After gelegenen Duftdrüsen. Die Tiere machen dabei einen regelrechten Handstand und drücken gleichzeitig den Beckenbereich reibend gegen den so zu markierenden Gegenstand. Ein Übermarkieren fremder Duftmarken, wie es der Haushund beim Beinheben zeigt, wurde bei den Kattas nicht beobachtet.

Auf der Innenseite der Unterarme liegen bei den Kattas haarlose dunkle Stellen. Es sind ebenfalls Duftdrüsenfelder, mit deren Hilfe ein Gegenstand durch Umklammern oder Reiben markiert werden kann. Besonders in den Morgenstunden, wenn die Tiere am aktivsten sind, gehen sie dazu in die Hockstellung und ziehen den nach vorn gerichteten Schwanz mehrmals durch diese Drüsenfelder, um ihn so zu imprägnieren.

Treffen sich dann zwei ranggleiche Kattas aus verschiedenen Familiengruppen, so gehen sie gemessenen Schrittes aufeinander zu, wobei der hoch aufgerichtete Schwanz wie ein Parfümwedel seitlich hin und her geschwenkt wird. Dadurch wird das optische Signal durch die Geruchsstoffe zusätzlich betont. Nach kurzem Nasenkontakt gehen dann die Tiere aneinander vorbei, wobei der in der Rangordnung tiefer stehende Katta die Wedelbewegungen früher einstellt als der Rivale. Nach einer solchen Begegnung kommt es sehr selten zu ernsten Streitigkeiten.

Kattas lieben – wie alle Lemuren – ausgiebige Sonnenbäder, wobei sie sich gerne in der Hockstellung mit dem Rücken an einen Felsen oder Baumstamm anlehnen. Die Arme ruhen dabei entweder lässig auf den Knien oder aber werden seitwärts ausgestreckt gehalten. So kann das Tier die wärmenden Sonnenstrahlen besonders genießen. Wegen dieses „Sonnenanbetens" werden Lemuren von abergläubischen Eingeborenen als Urwaldgespenster angesehen. Bekanntlich wird Goethes Faust von Lemuren (lat. „Gespenst") zu Grabe getragen.

3

Mit Giftpfeil und Blasrohr

Die Methode der Blasrohrjagd wurde von mehreren Kulturvölkern unabhängig voneinander entwickelt. So finden wir sie bei den südamerikanischen Indios ebenso verbreitet wie bei den Dajaks auf Borneo. Die Piaroa-Indianer vom Orinoko nutzen dazu das Carice-Rohr, das über 6 m lang knotenlos wächst. Das Mundstück wird mit Harz und Wachs angeklebt. Das fertige Blasrohr ist ein Präzisionsinstrument, mit dem Schüsse von 30–40 m möglich sind, und zu dem ein begehrtes Handelsobjekt. Die Giftpfeile werden aus den Blattrippen einer speziellen Palmenart hergestellt, als Stabilisatoren dienen fein gezwirnte Samenhaare von Pflanzen.

Die Treffergenauigkeit der ca. 40 cm langen, lautlosen Pfeile ist enorm. Das Pfeilgift wird in mehrfachen Schichten auf dem Pfeil aufgebracht, der zwischendurch am Feuer getrocknet wird. Ungefähr 2 cm hinter der Pfeilspitze macht der Jäger eine Einkerbung, damit der Pfeil an dieser Stelle abbricht und die vergiftete Pfeilspitze im Tierkörper stecken bleibt, wenn der Pfeil herausgezogen oder abgestreift wird. Mit Hilfe dieser lautlosen Jagdmethode ist es dem Indio möglich, aus einem Schwarm von Papageien oder einer Horde von Brüllaffen mehrere Tiere hintereinander zu erbeuten, ohne dass ein Abschussknall die restlichen verjagen würde. Beim Münchener Landesbeschussamt konnte durch Lichtschrankenmessung eine Geschwindigkeit von ca. 180 km/h des 1,5 g schweren Indiopfeils gemessen werden.

Die Gifte sind je nach Indiostamm verschieden. Besonders gefürchtet ist das Gift der Farbfrösche, deren Hautdrüsenfelder des Rückens bei Gefahr und Stress ein gallertiges Sekret absondern, das hochgiftig ist. So kann das Gift eines einzigen Frosches ausreichen, 20.000 Mäuse

oder 10 Menschen zu töten. Da Zoonachzuchten der Färberfrösche dieses hochaktive Gift nicht in ihrem Drüsensekret haben, nimmt man an, dass in freier Wildbahn mit dem Futter aufgenommene Bakterien für die Giftsynthese in Frage kommen.

gallertiges Giftsekret in Erregung

Aus Saft und Rinde des Brechnussbaumes (Strychnos nyx vomica) stellt ein anderer Indiostamm das bekannte Curare her, das nach Geheimrezepturen eingekocht wird, bevor es auf die Pfeile gestrichen werden kann. Beide Gifte haben eine nervenlähmende Wirkung und werden beim Verzehr im Magen-Darm-Kanal nicht resorbiert. Daher können die Jäger ihre Beute gefahrlos genießen.

Curare-Strauch

Originale Indio-Pfeil

Piaroa-Indio in Jagdtracht und Schusspositur

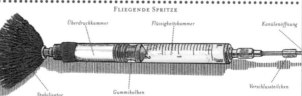

FLIEGENDE SPRITZE

Überdruckkammer — Flüssigkeitskammer — Kanülenöffnung

Stabilisator — Gummikolben — Verschlussteilchen

Der Giftpfeil, der im Zoo mit dem Telinject-Blasrohr-System verschossen wird, wiegt ca. 6 g und verlässt den Lauf bei einem guten Schützen mit ca. 92 km/h. In der Überdruckkammer ist gepresste Luft, welche den schwarzen Kolben und damit den Inhalt der Flüssigkeitskammer nach vorne treibt, wenn durch die Auftreffwucht das Verschlussteilchen von der Musku-

latur des Tierkörpers zurückgeschoben und die Öffnung der Injektionskanüle freigegeben wird. Die Flüssigkeitskammer wird nach Art und Gewicht des Tieres z.B. mit „Hellabrunner Mischung" gefüllt und kann wie eine Spritze mehrfach benutzt werden. Je nach Geschicklichkeit und Übungsstand des Schützen kann z.B. so ein Rothirsch bis auf 20 m Entfernung schmerzlos ins Reich der

Träume geschickt werden. Mit dem Blasrohrgewehr, in dessen Handgriff CO_2-Kapseln eingebaut sind, sind Schüsse von ca. 60 m mit erstaunlicher Treffsicherheit gewährleistet.

„Hellabrunner Mischung"

4

5

6

5–6
From *Müssen Tiere Zähne Putzen*. Mattei brings a highly original graphic approach to the communication of scientific and zoological information.

geoff waring

Geoff Waring is a graphic designer by training who has worked in magazine publishing for over 20 years. He is currently Art Director at Condé Nast's *Easy Living* magazine. As a child in the UK, his interests spread across birds, insects and the theatre, both his parents being actors. 'I was dragged around provincial theatres for many years. I loved it, but I was most interested in the set designs and the models made by the designers.' As a young art student, he applied to study illustration after his Foundation course but was unable to gain a place. After a year spent working as a junior in magazine design he was accepted to study Graphic Design at Manchester Polytechnic. Waring has held posts as art director at a number of publications including *Elle*, *Red* and *Vogue Australia*. The latter job played a key role in the development of the *Oscar* books. The real Oskar (as he was spelt) had to be left behind in London for Waring's move to Australia. Oscar was immortalized as the curious cat in the series of books that introduces children to various scientific concepts. The idea for the books as a way into science for children grew over a period of time and was eventually taken to Walker Books, who publish the series. Waring is passionate about the educational value of books and particularly about the need to excite children about the wonders of science: 'I was always looking under stones or up into the trees as a child. I'm not a scientist, I'm an artist, but I think if you can get children to learn about science you might be able to save the world. Good science can probably dig us out of the hole that we've got ourselves into. Very few kids are leaving school to go into science now.'

As a designer, his input on this side has been a key factor in the development of the overall look of the *Oscar* books, but he works closely with the designers at Walker too. 'Ironically, I'm not the greatest fan of computers. The books are created in Adobe InDesign, which is not really an illustration programme, so the process is quite crude.' He doesn't see books of the future as necessarily digitally created: 'I'm not sure that I want to work at a screen for the next 30 years. I draw with a chinagraph pencil in the early stages of the design and I can see this being used more in the future. If I were to hang any of my work on the wall, it would be the drawings.'

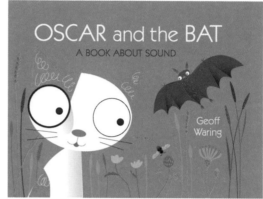

1

2

1–2
Front and back cover of *Oscar and the Bat* (Walker Books, 2006).

3–4
From *Oscar and the Bat*. Waring uses the curiosity of his character, Oscar, as a narrative thread to weave around simple scientific concepts. Through a series of books, Oscar the cat introduces children to the scientific concepts of light, sound and movement.

One summer evening, in the meadow, Oscar heard a new sound. He looked around. Who was making it?

Bat swooped by.
"It's the baby blackbirds," he said. "Their nest is over there in the bush."
"Oh," said Oscar. "I can hear them, even though I can't see them!"
"Yes," said Bat. "Our ears help us know what's around us, even when our eyes don't."

Cheep. cheep. cheep. cheep. cheep

3

"Kittens can make other sounds," Bat said. "So can bats!"

Squeak

Miaow

"We make sounds in our throats," Bat went on, "but some animals talk with different parts of their bodies."

Many male grasshoppers make sounds to female grasshoppers by rubbing their wings together.

Churrah chirp

Some cockroaches make sounds to one another through holes along their sides.

When they nest, some male hummingbirds make a loud sound with their wings to warn other birds away.

Bottlenose dolphins send messages to each other underwater through their blowholes.

Rattle. rattle

The tips of rattlesnakes' tails have hard connecting ridges. If other animals come too close, they lift and shake them.

4

"Are all sounds 'talking sounds'?" Oscar asked.
"Lots are," Bat said, "but nearly everything makes
a sound when it moves. Close your eyes and
listen. What can you hear moving
in the meadow?"

Grass makes no sound
when it's still, but it
swishes when the
wind moves it.

Swish
Swish
Swish
Swish
Swish
Swish

Machines are still and silent
until they are switched on.
Then their engines move
and make noises.

Brroooom

Still water in a pond is silent,
but moving water makes sounds.

Gurgle,
gurgle
Gurgle,
gurgle
Gurgle,
gurgle

12   13

5

Rumble, *rumble* *Rumble,* *rumble*

Oscar could hear another sound. It was in the sky.
"What's that rumbling?" he asked.

"Thunder," said Bat. "There's a storm coming.
Even though it's far away, we can still hear
the thunder because it's such a big sound."

Rumble, rumble   Rumble, rumble   Rumble, rumble

Oscar opened his eyes. "It's getting louder!" he said.

"The thunder's coming this way," Bat said.
"The closer it is to us, the louder it sounds to us…

14

6

5–8
Further spreads from *Oscar and
the Bat*. Waring's flat, digitally
rendered images bear the
hallmarks of an experienced
designer – elegantly balanced
shapes and colours cleverly
evoking the world of sound.

Safe under the leaves, Oscar listened to raindrops falling. "The rain is very near too," he said, "but it isn't scary."

"The rain is making a soft sound," Bat said, "not a harsh sound like the thunder."

18

19

7

When the rain stopped, Oscar put out his head to listen. "Is the thunder going away now?" he asked.

"Yes," said Bat. "The further it is from us, the quieter it sounds to us."

Then it was gone.
"I can't hear anything," Oscar whispered.
"No," whispered Bat. "This is silence – or it would be, if we weren't whispering!"

But just then...

21

8

Credits and contacts

Ragnar Aalbu
Perler For Svin. Illustrations © Ragnar Aalbu. Written by Helene Uri. Published by Mangschou, 2006.

Grundig Om Gris. Illustrations © Ragnar Aalbu. Written by Ragnar Aalbu. Published by Cappelen, 2005.

Brian Biggs
Illustrations from *Shredderman* and *Un Mode de Transport* reproduced by permission of the artist.

Serge Bloch
Illustrations reproduced by permission of the artist.

Marc Boutavant
Le Tour du Monde de Mouk. Author and illustrator: Marc Boutavant. Publisher: Editions Albin Michel Jeunesse.

Mouk s'Ennuie un Peu. Author and illustrator: Marc Boutavant. Publisher: Editions Mila.

Le Sapin. Author: Andersen. Illustrator: Marc Boutavant. Publisher: Nathan Jeunesse. Translation: Jean-Baptiste Coursaud.

Abracadabra. Author: Marc Boutavant. Publisher: Djeco.

Alexis Deacon
Illustrations © Alexis Deacon, 2004, from *Jitterbug Jam* by Barbara Jean Hicks and Alexis Deacon.

Illustrations © Alexis Deacon, 2006, from *While You Are Sleeping* by Alexis Deacon.

Both published by Hutchinson, an imprint of Random House Children's Books.

Lisa Evans
The Flower © Lisa Evans. Reproduced by permission of the artist.

Sara Fanelli
Illustrations © 2003 Sara Fanelli. From *Pinocchio* by Carlo Collodi, translated by Emma Rose and illustrated by Sara Fanelli. Reproduced by permission of Walker Books Ltd, London, SE11 5HJ.

Jeff Fisher
The Hair Scare and *Pass the Celery, Ellery!* © Jeff Fisher. Reproduced by permission of the artist.

Jason Ford
Art Auction Mystery. Concept © Anna Nilsen. Illustrations © Jason Ford, 2005. Copyright © Kingfisher Publications Plc, 2005. Art Director: Mike Davis.

Pieter Gaudesaboos
Roodlapje © Pieter Gaudesaboos and Uitgeverij Lannoo.

Stian Hole
Garmanns Sommer and *Den Gamle Mannen Og Hvalen* © Stian Hole.

David Hughes
Illustrations from *Cool Cat, Hot Dog* reproduced by permission of the artist.

The Hunchback of Notre Dame. Illustrations © David Hughes. From *The Hunchback of Notre Dame* by Victor Hugo, translated and adapted by Jan Needle and illustrated by David Hughes. Reproduced by permission of Walker Books Ltd, London SE11 5HJ.

Martin Jarrie
Illustrations reproduced by permission of the artist.

Meng-Chia Lai
Oh! © 2006, Meng-Chia Lai and Lirabelle. All rights reserved, in all countries. No copy permitted, whatever the process, without prior authorisation from the editor. Printed by Delta Colour (Nimes) and bound by la Sirc (Marigny le Chatel) on this first semester. The inital print run was 1500 copies.

Neal Layton
Illustrations © Neal Layton. From *Poo* by Nicola Davies and illustrated by Neal Layton. Reproduced by permission of Walker Books Ltd, London SE11 5HJ.

Gunter Mattei
Müssen Tiere Zähne Putzen? © Carl Hanser Verlag München Wien 2005.

Das große Buch der Tiere © Carl Hanser Verlag München Wien 2006.

David Merveille
Le Jacquot De Monsieur Hulot. Editions du Rouergue.

Paula Metcalf
Illustrations © Paula Metcalf, 2005. From *Mabel's Magical Garden*, published by Macmillan Children's Books.

Taro Miura
Illustrations reproduced by permission of the artist.

Toby Morison
Little Louis Takes Off. Illustrations by Toby Morison. © Simon & Schuster UK. Book designed by Genevieve Webster.

Elena Odriozola
Fin © Elena Odriozola and Alejandro Fernández.

Story of Noah © Elena Odriozola and Meadowside Children's Books.

Begira Begira © Elena Odriozola and Elkar.

Kvĕta Pacovská
Flying © Kvĕta Pacovská.

Maurizio Quarello
Marizul, que Suena © OQO Editora S.L. 2006. Text: Bernardino Rivadavia. Illustrations: Maurizio A. C. Quarello. Graphic Design: OQOMANIA. First Edition: June 2006. ISBN: 8496573478

Babau Cerca Casa © Orecchio Acerbo Srl, 2005. Text: Maurizio A. C. Quarello. Illustrations: Maurizio A. C. Quarello. Graphic Design: Orecchio Acerbo. First Edition: September 2005. ISBN: 8889025255

Kristin Roskifte
Still Deg I Kø © Illustrations: Kristin Roskifte. Written by Kristin Roskifte. Published by Cappelen, 2005.

28 Rom Og Kjøkken © Illustrations: Kristin Roskifte. Written by Kristin Roskifte Published by Cappelen, 2004.

Harriet Russell
A is for Rhinoceros © 2005 Harriet Russell. All rights reserved to Maurizio Corraini srl.

A Colouring Book for the Lazy © 2006 Harriet Russell. All rights reserved to Maurizio Corraini srl.

Margarita Sada
Illustrations reproduced by permission of the artist.

Marina Sagona
Illustrations from *No* reproduced by permission of the artist and Orcecchi Arcerbo.

Istvan Schritter
Des Ronds et des Carrés. Written by Didier Mounié. Published by Motus, 1998.

Illustrations from *Todo el Dinero del Mundo* and *Avion que Va, Avion que Llega* reproduced by permission of the artist.

Boca de Leon published by E.D.B, 2006; *Leyenda Ugandesa* published by Tándem, 2000.

Ko Kyung Sook
Illustrations from *Magic Bottles* © Kyung Sook Ko.

Shaun Tan
The Red Tree published by Lothian/Hachette, 2001.

Øyvind Torseter
For En Neve Havre © Øyvind Torseter. Reproduced by permission of Cappelen, 2004.

Klikk © Øvind Torseter. Reproduced by permission of Cappelen.

Englefjell © Øvind Torseter. Reproduced by permission of Cappelen.

Isabelle Vandenabeele
Mijn Schaduw en Ik © 2005, Isabelle Vandenabeele, Wezestraat 30a, 8850 Ardooie, Belgium and Vitgevery De Eenhoorn, Vlasstraat 17, 8710 Wielsbeke, Belguim.

Rood Rood Roodkapje © 2003, Isabelle Vandenabeele, Wezestraat 30a, 8850 Ardooie, Belgium and Vitgevery De Eenhoorn, Vlasstraat 17, 8710 Wielsbeke, Belgium.

Noemí Villamuza
Libros de Nanas © Noemí Villamuza. Reproduced by permission of Media Vaca and also with permission of the artist.

Me Gusta © Noemí Villamuza. Reproduced by permission of Kokinos and also with permission of the artist.

Geoff Waring
Illustrations © 2006 Geoff Waring. From *Oscar and the Bat* by Geoff Waring. Reproduced by permission of Walker Books Ltd, London SE11 5HJ.

Morteza Zahedi
Roosters © Morteza Zahedi 2007. All Rights Reserved.

Genie Collection © Morteza Zahedi 2007. All Rights Reserved.

Butterfly Journey © Morteza Zahedi 2007. All Rights Reserved.

2 Turtles – 2 Humans © Morteza Zahedi 2007. All Rights Reserved.

Ragnar Aalbu
www.patron.no

Brian Biggs
www.mrbiggs.com

Serge Bloch
www.sergebloch.net

Marc Boutavant
c/o Heart Illustration Agency
www.heartagency.com

Alexis Deacon
www.randomhouse.co.uk

Lisa Evans
www.firefluff.blogspot.com

Sara Fanelli
www.sarafanelli.com

Jeff Fisher
www.rileyillustration.com

Jason Ford
c/o Heart Illustration Agency
www.heartagency.com

Pieter Gaudesaboos
www.gaudesaboos.be

Martin Jarrie
www.marlenaagency.com

Stian Hole
www.cappelen.no

David Hughes
www.davidhughesillustration.co.uk

Meng-Chia Lai
www.mengchialai.com

Neal Layton
www.neallayton.com

Günter Mattei
www.hanser.de

David Merveille
www.illustrateur.belgium/davidmerveille

Paula Metcalf
www.paulametcalf.co.uk

Taro Miura
www.taromiura.com

Toby Morison
c/o Heart Illustration Agency
www.heartagency.com

Elena Odriozola
www.pencil-illustradores.com

Kvĕta Pacovská
www.ricochet-jeunes.org

Maurizio Quarello
www.quarello.com

Kristin Roskifte
www.patron.no

Harriet Russell
www.harrietrussell.co.uk

Margarita Sada
www.edicionescastillo.com

Marina Sagona
www.rileyillustration.com

Istvan Schritter
www.istvan.com

J.otto Seibold
www.jottodotcom.com

Ko Kyung Sook
www.jaimimage.co.kr

Shaun Tan
www.shauntan.net

Øyvind Torseter
www.cappelen.no

Isabelle Vandenabeele
www.eenhorn.be

Noemí Villamuza
www.mediavaca.com

Geoff Waring
www.walkerbooks.co.uk

Morteza Zahedi
www.parkingallery.com